HISTORY OF ENGLAND,

In Verse,

FROM THE INVASION OF JULIUS CÆSAR TO THE PRESENT TIME.

WITH

ILLUSTRATIVE NOTES, CHRONOLOGICAL CHART OF THE KINGS OF ENGLAND, TABLES OF CONTEMPORARY SOVEREIGNS,

AND

A TABLE,

DESCRIPTIVE OF THE PRESENT CONDITION OF GREAT BRITAIN.

BY

HANNAH TOWNSEND.

PHILADELPHIA:
LINDSAY & BLAKISTON.
1852.

STEREOTYPED BY J. FAGAN. C. SHERMAN, PRINTER.

PREFACE.

THIS little work has been written under the impression that verse is generally more readily learned, and longer retained in the memory, than prose, and that, if the incidents in the History of England could be thus clearly, but briefly enumerated, the student would have in his mind a consecutive history, the minuter details of which he could supply by farther study.

Abstaining from mere kingly gossip, I have endeavoured to select those facts which are of *actual* importance — which have affected the nation, the people — which have indicated their progress in civilization, religion, commerce, literature, science, and art — to place cause and effect together, thus helping the student to think, and to condense as much as possible, that the memory may not be burdened with useless words. I hope the difficulty of this condensation, with the continual introduction of names, dates, and unrhythmical words and phrases, will serve as an apology to the reader, when his ear is annoyed by inharmonious verse; but, above all, I trust that nothing will be found which can poison the mind, that no seed will be implanted which may hereafter grow to bear bitter fruit.

I have endeavoured to remove the gloss from war—to speak against it when I could—and to distinguish between those conflicts which were aggressive, and productive of only military glory, and those which were an expression, though an unchristian one, of insulted manhood, for a maintenance of just rights.

PHILADELPHIA, 1852.

TABLE OF CONTENTS.

	Page.
Divisions of England in the Roman Period	7
Rulers of Britain during the Roman Period	8
Introduction	13
Egbert	20
Ethelwolf	20
Ethelbald. Ethelbert	21
Ethelred I.	21
Alfred	21
Edward the Elder	24
Athelstan. Edmund I.	25
Edred. Edwy	26
Edgar the Peaceable	26
Edward the Martyr	27
Ethelred II. Sweyn	28
Edmund II.	29
Canute	29
Harold I. Hardi-Canute	30
Edward the Confessor	30
Harold II.	32
William the Conqueror	33
William II.	37
Crusades	38
Henry I.	39
Stephen	41
Henry II.	43
Richard I.	48
John	50

PAGE.
HENRY III. 53
EDWARD I. 56
EDWARD II. 58
EDWARD III. 60
RICHARD II. 63
HENRY IV. 65
HENRY V. 67
HENRY VI. 68
EDWARD IV. 71
EDWARD V. 74
RICHARD III. 74
HENRY VII. 76
HENRY VIII. 79
EDWARD VI. 83
MARY 85
ELIZABETH 87
JAMES I. 91
CHARLES I. 95
THE COMMONWEALTH 99
CHARLES II. 102
JAMES II. 105
WILLIAM III. AND MARY 106
ANNE 108
GEORGE I. 111
GEORGE II. 113
GEORGE III. 116
GEORGE IV. 123
WILLIAM IV. 126
VICTORIA 128

REIGNING SOVEREIGNS OF EUROPE 133
SOVEREIGNS OF ENGLAND 136
STATISTICAL TABLES 142

DIVISION OF ENGLAND,

AT THE TIME OF THE ROMAN INVASION.

England, including Wales, was, at the invasion of the Romans, divided into the following seventeen states:—

CALLED BY THE ROMANS,	CONSISTING OF
1. THE DAMMONII.....	Cornwall and Devon.
2. DUROTRIGES........	Dorsetshire.
3. BELGÆ..............	Somersetshire, Wilts, and part of Hants.
4. ATTREBATTI........	Berkshire.
5. REGNI...............	Surrey, Sussex, and remaining part of Hants.
6. CANTII...............	Kent.
7. DOBUNI..............	Gloucester and Oxfordshire.
8. CATTICUCHLANI....	Bucks, Bedford, and Herts.
9. TRINOBANTES......	Essex and Middlesex.
10. ICENI.................	Suffolk, Norfolk, Huntingdon, and Cambridge.
11. CORITANI...........	Northampton, Leicester, Rutland, Lincoln, Nottingham, and Derby.
12. CORNARI............	Warwick, Worcester, Stafford, Chester, and Shropshire.
13. THE SILURES......	Radnor, Brecon, Glamorgan, Monmouth, and Hereford.
14. DEMETÆ............	Pembroke, Cardigan, and Caermathon.
15. ORDOVICES.........	Montgomery, Merioneth, Caernarvon, Flint, and Denbigh.
16. THE BRIGANTES...	York, Durham, Lancashire, Westmoreland, and Cumberland.
17. OTTADINI..........	Northumberland to the Sweed.

RULERS OF BRITAIN,

FROM THE INVASION OF JULIUS CÆSAR TO THE DEPARTURE OF THE ROMANS.

		B. C.
1.	Cassivelaunus	83
2.	Theomantius	50
3.	Cymbeline	24
		A. D.
4.	Guiderius	45
5.	Arniagus	73
6.	Marius	125
7.	Coilus	179
8.	Lucius	207
9.	Severus (Emperor)	211
10.	Bassianus	218
11.	Carausius	225
12.	Alectus	232
13.	Asclepiodorus	262
14.	Coilus II.	289
15.	Constantius (Emperor)	310
16.	Constantine (Emperor)	329

FROM THE DEPARTURE OF THE ROMANS TILL THE INTRODUCTION OF THE SAXONS BY VORTIGERN.

		A. D.
1.	Octavius	383
2.	Maximiniamus	391
3.	Gratian	431
4.	Constantine I.	446
5.	Constantius	446
6.	Vortigern	450

HISTORY OF ENGLAND,

In Verse.

FROM THE ROMAN INVASION TO THE END OF THE SAXON HEPTARCHY.

B. C. 55—A. D. 827. 882 YEARS.

FROM *Tan*, a country, and *Breit*, tin,
The name of Britain came,*
And only as the *Land of Tin*,
Was it first known to fame.†

'T was peopled by the Celts and Gaels‡
In time to us unknown,
Its history preserved in song
Of Cambrian bards alone.§

---

* Pictorial History of England.

† The Phœnicians traded very early with the inhabitants of Cornwall for copper and tin; but they were unacquainted with the interior of the country.

‡ A colony from Gaul, (the ancient France.) Their descendants are chiefly in Wales, the highlands of Scotland, and the north of Ireland. They are still a distinct race, speaking the language of their remote ancestors.—*McCulloch.*

§ Pliny.—The earliest *authentic* history commences with the invasion by Julius Cæsar, B. C. 55.

B. C. 55. Cæsar, before Christ fifty-five,
Anchored upon its strand,
And found a people clad in skins*
Inhabiting the land.

Bravely by Cassibe'lan led,†
Did they resist his will;
But their rude warfare could not cope
With Roman arms and skill.

B. C. 43. Rome from the conquest little gained
Until, in forty-three,
Ostorius‡ went, and o'er the kings
Obtained a victory.

Caractacus, the chieftain brave,
Who last in arms remained,

---

* Their arms and legs were uncovered, and were usually painted blue. Their long hair flowed over their shoulders; but their beards, excepting on the upper lip, were closely cut. Plutarch says they were so habitually regular and temperate, that they only began to grow old at a hundred and twenty years.

† Mentioned by the early historians as the first British general who opposed the Romans. The name is variously written. *Cassibealau'nus, Cassivelau'nus*, and *Cassibe'lan.* "Cæsar relates that Cassivelau'nus, after dismissing all his other forces, retained no fewer than 4000 war-chariots about his person. These chariots had short scythes attached to the axle-trees, which inflicted terrible wounds." — *Haydn.*

‡ In the reign of the emperor Claudius.

Was sent to Rome, and, with his wife,
Walked through the city, chained.*

But still the Britons, unsubdued,
Arose, the foe to meet;
'Till Nero sent Suetonius
The conquest to complete.

The Druids† o'er the people held
An undisputed sway;
Priests, poets, and historians,
And magistrates, were they.

In caves they lived, on berries fed,
Were strict in faith and life;
They urged the Britons to revolt,
And led them in the strife.

---

* It is related of Caractacus, that, looking around upon the costly splendour of the city, he exclaimed, "How is it possible that men possessed of such magnificence at home, should envy Caractacus an humble cottage in Britain?"

† A celebrated order among the ancient Germans, Gauls, and Britons, who were so called from their veneration for the oak (Drys). In England, they were chosen from the best families, that the dignity of their birth, added to that of their station, might procure them the greater respect. *Rowland's Mona Antiqua.*—They worshipped in the open air; and there remain in England circles of stone laid upon the ground, which it is supposed enclosed their sanctuaries. The mistletoe, a parasitic plant, was used in their rites, and venerated as a symbol of their faith. *Mrs. Markham.*—They sacrificed human victims, which they burned in large wicker idols.

Sue′tonius doomed them unto death,
Wherever they were seen,
And conquered Boadi′cea,
Ice′ni's hero queen.

Upon that bloody field of war
His slaughtered thousands lay;
Then Britain, broken-hearted, bowed
Beneath the Roman sway.

Agric′ola next went, and taught
The useful arts of life;
But with the Caledonians waged*
A fierce and deadly strife.

He built a chain of forts across,
From Solway Frith to Clyde,
To keep the bold, free-hearted chiefs
Upon the northern side.

The Emperor Ad′rian raised a wall
Composed of turf alone;
And afterward Antonius
Made one of earth and stone.

---

* Caledonia — Scotland. The name is supposed to be derived from Gael or Gaelmen, or Gadel-doine, corrupted by the Romans.—*Haydn.*

At length Seve'rus, who resolved
  The enemy should yield,
Went thither in two hundred seven,
  But could not gain the field:

His army built another wall
  From Solway Frith to Tyne;
But still the Caledonians waged
  Fierce war beyond the line.

The Romans left the British Isles
  Four hundred and fourteen,
But still remains of roads and walls,
  And villas, can be seen.

Next came the Scots and Picts,* and spread
  Rapine and ruin far;
The Britons called the Saxon chiefs
  To aid them in the war:

448–460. They came, and fought the Scots and Picts,
  But conquered Britain, too;
From *Angle*, a famed Saxon tribe,
  The name of England grew.†

---

* The name by which the inhabitants of Scotland were at that time distinguished. The Picts, so called from *Pictich*, a plunderer, and the Scots, from *Scuite*, a wanderer, in the Celtic tongue, were only different tribes of Caledonians. — *Dr. Henry*.

† The national appellation of Britons in time gave place to that of Anglo-Saxons, the latter signifying Saxons born in England. A

Each Saxon chief kept for himself
  The land torn from his foes;
And thus the Saxon Heptarchy
  On Britain's ruins rose.

The Romans first the Druids killed,
  And brought the Christian faith,
And now the Saxons persecute
  The Christians unto death.

Some of the Britons fled to Wales,
  And hid in mountains lone,
And others to the north of France,
  As Brittany now known.

Arthur, the prince of the Silures,
  Opposed the Saxon might —
His knights of the Round Table fought
  Full many a desperate fight.

Among the Saxons were five ranks —
  First *Kings*, and second *Earls*,
Freemen the third, each to some lord
  Attached, and named the *Ceorls*.

The fourth, *ignoble Ceorls*, were sold,
  Or given with the land;

---

history of the Anglo-Saxons, relates to the people who inhabited England from the Saxon to the Norman invasion. — *Mrs. Markham.*

The fifth were *theowes*, or full slaves,
  Sold at the market stand.*

Gildas, of Wales, surnamed "The Wise,"
  The oldest writer known,
Among the British people lived,
  Five hundred sixty-one.

The "Venerable Bede" was born
  Six hundred seventy-three,
And unto him the English owe
  Their first church history.

Adhelm, renowned as the first bard
  Who English ballads wrote,
Lived in six hundred ninety-eight,
  A linguist he of note.

Then Caedmon† lived, and Alcuin,‡
  Who Saxon poets were;
And Nennius, an historian,
  Who died eight hundred four.

---

* Even little children were carried to Rome and exposed in the public markets for sale, and this led to the first Christian mission upon record. A. D. 596, Gregory, observing the extreme beauty of some of these children, observed, "They would have been angels, had they been Christians." And when he afterwards became Pope, he sent St. Augustine, with forty monks, to redeem Britain from paganism.

† Died 600.

‡ Died 600. Also wrote on history and theology.

SAXON KINGS.—17.

EGBERT — FIRST SOLE MONARCH OF ENGLAND.

827—838. 11 YEARS.

827. Eight hundred twenty-seven saw
The Heptarchy* o'erthrown,
And Egbert, the first sovereign
Of England, reigned alone.

Then from the north came forth the Danes,
And overran the land;
But they were driven out with loss,
Twice by King Egbert's hand.

ETH'ELWOLF.

838—857. 19 YEARS.

King Eth'elwolf repulsed the Danes;
He granted tythes to priests,
And gave them from all services
And imposts, a release.

* Heptarchy — seven kingdoms.

ETH'ELBALD. ETH'ELBERT. ETH'ELRED I.

857—872. 15 YEARS.

Next Eth'elbald and Eth'elbert
Ruled jointly, and their reigns
Lasted nine years. Then Eth'elred,
Who died fighting the Danes.

CONTEMPORARY SOVEREIGNS.

Popes.	A. D.	Emperors of the East.	A. D.	Kings of Scotland.	A. D.
Gregory IV.	823	Michael II.	821	Congallus III.	824
Sergius II.	844	Theophilus I.	829	Dongallus	829
Leo IV.	847	Michael III.	842	Alpinus	834
Benedict III.	855	**Emperors of the West and Kings of France.**		Kennethus II.	849
Nicholas I.	858	Lewis I.	814	Donaldus	859
John VIII.	872	Lotharius	840	Constantius	865
		Lewis II.	855		

ALFRED THE GREAT.

872—900. 28 YEARS.

'Twas in eight hundred seventy-two
Great Alfred gained the throne,

Lenient, yet just, learned,* wise, and good,
His people's cause his own.†

He fought the Danes, and conquered them,
Then changed the foe to friend;
He gave them land, and all the aid
His kingly power could lend.

The English navy he commenced;
But what was better far,
He taught his people they should live
For peace, and not for war.

So for the Saxon, who required,
To pass the weary time,
The fight, the hunt, the game of chess,
Or wandering gleeman's rhyme,

---

* The following extract from the Lord's Prayer, translated by Alfred, will give an idea of the language then spoken in England: Faeder ure thu the earth on heafenum, si thin nama gehalgod, to becume thin rice, Gewurthe hin willa on earthen swa swa on heafenum urne ge daegwanlican hlaf syle us to daeg, and forgyf us ure gyltas, swa swa we forgivath urum gyltendum, and ne geladde thu us on consenung ac alyse us of yfle. (Si it swa.)

† King Alfred endeavoured to impress this principle upon the mind of his son and successor. Calling him to his side when he felt his last moments approaching, he said, "My son, be thou the children's father and the widow's friend. Comfort thou the poor, shelter the weak, and, with all thy might, right that which is wrong."

He built the University
  Of Oxford, pledging then
Places in Church and Government
  Only to learned men.

He framed a code of laws,* enforced
  The jury trial, too,†
And founded schools, where landed men
  Must send, or pay the due.

The kingdom into counties was
  Divided in this reign;‡
Markets and fairs were introduced,
  As readier means of gain.§

Houses of wood alone were seen,
  Stone but in churches found,
But the first Christian church was built
  Of wattles, interwound.

---

* This code is lost; but it is supposed to have been the origin of the common law.

† The introduction of the jury trial is usually attributed to Alfred; but Phillips says that there is evidence of a case having been tried at Hawarden nearly a hundred years before his reign. The list of the twelve jurors is preserved.

‡ It was divided into *counties, hundreds,* and *tithings.* County courts were held monthly, and became the great safeguard of the civil rights of Englishmen.

§ Coined money was not used; everything was bought and sold by barter.

Few were the learned men; but first
Were Eth'elwald* and Asser,†
J. Scotus Erigina,‡ too,
The famed philosopher.

CONTEMPORARY SOVEREIGNS.

Popes.	A. D.	Emperors of the West and Kings of France.	A. D.	Kings of Scotland.	A. D.
John VIII.	872	Lewis II.	855	Constantine II.	863
Martin II.	882	Charles I.	873	Ethus	878
Adrian III.	884	Charles II.	880	Gregory	880
Stephen VI.	885	Arnold	888	Donaldson VI.	898
Formosus	891	Lewis III.	899		
Emperors of the East.					
Basilius I.	867				
Leo VI.	886				

EDWARD THE ELDER.

900—925. 25 YEARS.

Edward the Elder wisely ruled;
He oft repulsed the Dane;
The Cambridge University
Was founded in his reign.

---

* Died 900. Wrote "History of Great Britain."

† Died 909. Wrote "History of England," and "Life of Alfred."

‡ Died 883. Wrote a philosophical work, entitled "Of the Nature of Things." His theological views are said to have been similar to Luther's.

ATH'ELSTAN. EDMUND I.

925—948. 23 YEARS.

An able king was Ath'elstan,
And popular his reign;
He fought and conquered Irish, Welsh,
Northumbrian, Scot and Dane.

The Scriptures were translated then
Into the Saxon tongue;
And, as a *title*, was conferred
The name of gentleman—

On every merchant who had been
Twice to the midland sea.*
Next Edmund First was crowned the king;
But a short reign had he;

For Leolf in the monarch's blood
His robber hands imbrued.
In this, and the succeeding reign,
The Danes the war renewed.

* The Mediterranean—at that time called Midland Sea.

EDRED. EDWY.

948—959. 11 YEARS.

Edred was bigoted and weak,
The dupe of Dunstan's art.
Dunstan and Odo killed the queen,
Dear unto Edwy's heart.

And when, excited by these priests,
His brother Edgar tried
To seize upon his throne, he drooped,
And, broken-hearted, died.

EDGAR THE PEACEABLE.

959—975. 16 YEARS.

King Edgar, by wise government,
Subdued the robber bands;
No wars he made, but killed the wolves*
Infesting all the lands.

* Their heads were demanded as a tribute (particularly three hundred yearly from Wales) by King Edgar, A. D. 961, by which step they were totally destroyed. — *Carte.*

CONTEMPORARY SOVEREIGNS.

Popes.	A. D.		A. D.		A. D
Benedict IV.	900	John XIII.	965	Henry I.	919
Leo V.	904	Benedict VI.	972	Otho I.	936
Sergius III.	905	Donus	972	Otho II.	973
Anastasius III.	910	**Emperors of the East.**		**Kings of France.**	
Lando	912	Leo VI.	886	Charles III.	899
John X.	913	Constantine Porphyrogenitus	910	Lewis IV.	936
Leo VI.	928	Romanus the Younger	959	Lothaire I.	954
Stephen VIII.	929	Nicephorus	963	**Kings of Scotland.**	
John XI.	931	Zimisces	970	Constantine III.	909
Leo VII.	936	**Emperors of the West.**		Malcolm I.	943
Stephen IX.	939	Lewis IV.	899	Indulphus	958
Martin II.	943	Conrade I.	912	Duffus	967
Agapet II.	950			Culenus	972
John XII.	956				
Benedict V.	964				

EDWARD THE MARTYR.

975—978. 3 YEARS.

Edward, surnamed the Martyr, was
 Gentle and kind to each;
And yet his wicked step-mother
 Met him with courteous speech,

And proffered wine; and as he drank,
 Unconscious of her art,
A servant, by her orders, thrust
 A dagger to his heart.

ETH'ELRED II., THE UNREADY. SWEYN (DANE).

978—1016. 38 YEARS.

The second Ethelred was ne'er
  Prepared to meet the Danes;
He gave them bribes to leave the land,
  Again and yet again;

And to procure this fund, imposed
  A tax which was abhorred,
Called *Danegelt*, which remained until
  The Saxon line restored.

He wed a Norman* princess, thus
  Securing Norman aid;
But in revenge of former wrongs,
  A massacre was made

Of all the Danes throughout the land;
  And when the act was known,
Sweyn, who was king of Norway,† came
  And seized upon the throne.

---

* Normandy (situated in the north of France) was anciently called Neustria. It was granted by the king of France to duke Rollo and his Normans (Northmen); hence Normandy. — *Putnam.*

† The Norwegians were also called Danes.

Ethelred fled to Normandy;
  But King Sweyn dying soon,
He came back, fought the Danes, and left
  The kingdom to his son.

EDMUND II., IRONSIDE.

1016—1017. 1 YEAR.

Edmund the Second (Ironside)
  Oft battled with the Dane;
Then with Canute parted the crown,
  But was soon after slain.

DANISH KINGS.—3.

CANUTE THE GREAT.

1017—1036. 19 YEARS.

Canute the Great was crowned; and thus,
  Aftor two centuries passed
In fighting with and conquering Danes,
  A Dane was king at last.

And he was thought the greatest king
Reigning in Europe then;
Wise laws he made, and patronized
Letters and learned men.

He sent his fleet and army back,
To make it clearly known,
He felt himself secure with them,
And safe upon their throne.

HAROLD I., HAREFOOT. HARDI-CANUTE.

1036—1041. 5 YEARS.

Harold his son succeeded him;
His chief joy was the chase;
Hardi-Canute, his brother, next,
Last of the Danish race.

SAXON LINE RESTORED.

EDWARD THE CONFESSOR.

1041—1066. 25 YEARS.

Weary at length of Danish kings,
The greatest joy was shown

When Edward, "the Confessor" styled,
  Received the proffered throne.

He was the son of Eth'elred,
  And of his Norman wife,
And in a Norman monastery
  Thus far had passed his life.

He introduced the Norman dress,
  And spoke the Norman tongue;*
The Norman baron's haughty tread
  Throughout his palace rung.

He exiled Godwin and his sons,
  Because they frowned on this,
And gave their broad and fertile lands
  To Norman favourites.

But with a fleet they soon returned,
  Demanding lands and right;
They conquered, and the Normans fled
  The country in affright.

The people thought that Edward's touch
  The scrofula would cure;
And the kings touched for this disease
  Six hundred years and more.

---

* The language used by the Saxons in England was the Norman-Saxon. The Normans introduced the Norman-French; and the Latin, previously introduced by the Romans, was used in the churches. The present English is a mixture of Anglo-Saxon, Norman-French, and Latin.

HAROLD II.

1066—1066.

When Edward died, Earl Godwin's son,
   Harold, usurped the throne;
He was the last of Saxon blood
   That ever sat thereon —

Nor reigned he very long, before
   The Norman William came,
In right, he said, of Edward's will,
   The English crown to claim:

And in ten hundred sixty-six,
   October, fourteenth day,
They fought at Hastings; and the land
   Passed to the Norman sway.*

* At the time of the Norman invasion, nearly a third of the land is said to have belonged to monasteries, nunneries, and the clergy; and this is supposed to have been one great cause of the duke of Normandy's easy victory." — *Mrs. Markham.*

There is still preserved in the town-house of Rouen, a curious monument of antiquity, called the Bayeux Tapestry, embroidered by Matilda, queen of William the First. It represents *all the facts of the conquest*, commencing with the visit of Harold at the Norman court, and ending with the crowning of William, 1066. It is divided into compartments, and is 214 feet long and 19 inches wide.

CONTEMPORARY SOVEREIGNS.

Popes.	A. D.
Benedict VII. ..	975
John XIV.	984
John XV.	985
Gregory V......	996
Silvester II.	999
John XVI.	1003
John XVII.	1004
Sergius IV......	1009
Benedict VIII. ..	1012
John XVIII.....	1024
Benedict IX.....	1033
Gregory VI.	1044
Clement II.	1046
Damascus II. ...	1048
Leo IX.	1049
Victor II.	1055
Stephen X......	1057
Nicholas II.	1059
Alexander II....	1061

Emperors of the East.	A. D.
Basilius II......	975
Constantine X...	1025
Romanus III....	1028
Michael IV.....	1034
Michael V......	1041
Constantine XI..	1042
Theodore (emp.)	1054
Michael VI.....	1056
Isaac Comnenus	1059
Constantine XII.	1059

Emperors of the West.	
Otho II.........	973
Otho III........	983
Henry II.	1002
Conrad II.	1024
Henry III.	1039
Henry IV.	1056

Kings of France.	A. D.
Lothaire	954
Louis V.	986
Hugh Capet....	987
Robert II.	997
Henry I.	1031
Philip I.	1060

Kings of Scotland.	
Culenus	972
Kenneth III.....	977
Constantine IV..	1002
Gremius	1005
Malcolm II.	1054
Duncan I.......	1031
Macbeth.......	1043
Malcolm III. ...	1057

NORMAN FAMILY.—3.

WILLIAM THE CONQUEROR.

1066—1087. 21 YEARS.

Though William, styled "the Conqueror,"
Had gained the English throne,

The people still were resolute
  Saxons should rule alone.

They saw the Normans growing rich
  On lands which they had tilled,
And offices in church and state
  By Normans only filled.

In every court and school did they
  The Norman language hear;
And in the service of the church
  It grated on their ear.

The surname then was introduced
  By Normans who had come,
Adding unto their Christian name
  That of their early home.

William permitted game to be
  Killed only by his hand;
And thirty villages he burned,
  For the "New Forest" land.*

And any one who killed a beast
  That in that Forest ran,
Suffered a heavier penalty
  Than he who slew a man.

---

* He dispeopled the country for thirty miles round.— *Stowe.*

He introduced the feudal laws,*
 Compiled the "Doomsday-book,"†
And France invaded, burning all
 The villages he took.

---

* Feudal, from the modern Latin word *feodum* or *feud*; in English, *fief* or fee. — *Brande.* Under the feudal system, the land was held by military tenure — that is, military service was the compensation, or rent, paid for it. It was divided by the king among the barons, who were to be prepared to follow him to battle whenever he should require it. By the barons it was again divided among the peasantry, the vassals, or *retainers*, as they were called, who were expected to attend them upon all their warlike excursions; which in those days, when each feudal chieftain was a sort of petty king, when each was jealous of the other, and when war was the great *business* of life, were very frequent. The chiefs lived not in pleasant houses, built for comfort and convenience, but in great gloomy castles, contrived only for warlike defence. The vassals were required to build these castles, and garrison them; to build the churches, and to attend their lords, not only in war, but in their visits to neighbouring castles, acting as their body-guards, and forming what was called their retinue. When men began to pay more attention to letters, to learn to till the ground, to study the art of clothing their neighbours rather than the art of killing them, the feudal system began to disappear; but it was not annihilated until the *common* men began to be respected, until they were considered not as mere appendages to their lords, but as independent, responsible beings, who had rights, inalienable rights, which ought to be respected and maintained. With the cultivation of the gentle arts of peace, the elevation of the masses, and the consequent restricted power of the aristocracy, the feudal system disappeared.

† It contains a description of every landed estate throughout England, (excepting in the counties of Northumberland and Durham); the character of its soil, its productions, the cattle with which it was

The jury trial he exchanged
For that of single fight;*
At eight was rung the curfew-bell,
To put out fire and light.

The ignorant and poor he scorned;
To letters gave his aid;
Ingulphus† honoured, and the learned
Lanfranc‡ archbishop made.

CONTEMPORARY SOVEREIGNS.

Popes.	A. D.		A. D.	King of France.	A. D.
Alexander II....	1061	Romanus IV....	1063	Philip I........	1060
Gregory VII.....	1073	Michael VII....	1071		
Victor III.	1086	Nicephorus I....	1078	**Kings of Scotland.**	
		Alexis I........	1081	Malcolm III.	1059
Emperors of the East.		**Emperor of the West.**		Donald VIII....	1068
Constantine XII.	1059	Henry IV.......	1056		

---

stocked, the name of its proprietor, and its monied value. "This domes-day book was the tax book of Kinge William." — *Camden.* It is still preserved in the Exchequer, and may be consulted by those who are anxious to learn to whom their lands belonged at the time of the Conquest.

* In the trial by single combat, the victor was always considered the innocent person.

† Secretary to William the First, and his historian.

‡ Archbishop of Canterbury.

WILLIAM II., RUFUS.

1087—1100. 13 YEARS.

King Rufus built Westminster Hall,
The London bridge and Tower,
And banished Anselm,* who maintained
The Pope supreme in power.

The Norway king made a descent
On England in this reign,
Ten hundred ninety-eight, the last
Invasion of the Dane.

CONTEMPORARY SOVEREIGNS.

Popes.	A. D.	Emperor of the East.	A. D.	King of France.	A. D.
Victor III.	1086	Alexis I.	1081	Philip I.	1060
Urban II.	1088				
Pascal II.	1099	**Emperor of the West.**		**King of Scotland.**	
		Henry IV.	1056	Donald VIII.	1068

* Archbishop of Canterbury.

CRUSADES.*

1096—1291. 195 YEARS.

The year ten hundred ninety-six
  Witnessed the first Crusade;
Pope Gregory planned it, and besought
  Peter the Hermit's aid.

And that his tomb, who was the Prince
  Of *Peace*, might not remain
With those who trusted not in him,
  Six million men were slain!

Two million men from Europe went
  To join the holy war;†
And for two hundred fifty years
  Blood flowed on Syria's shore.

---

* These wars were called *Crusades*, because a figure of the cross was the badge of the warrior. It surmounted the staff upon which he leaned; was painted upon his banner; engraved upon his shield, and embroidered upon his garments. He carried with him a *scrip*, or bag for food, and a *scallop-shell*, attached to the front of his cap, which served him for a drinking-cup. These warriors were called *Crusaders*, *Pilgrims*, or *Palmers*. The last name originated from the practice usual amongst them, of bringing with them on their return branches of *palm*. The palm is an emblem of victory; and being a tree peculiar to the country, it was an additional proof of their having been there.

† It seemed as though all Europe had emptied itself upon Asia.—*Anna Comnena.*

HENRY I., BEAUCLERC.*

BEGAN TO REIGN AUGUST 5TH, 1100. REIGNED 35 YEARS.

Henry the First, in those dark days
For varied learning known,
Upon King William Rufus' death,
Usurped the vacant throne.

He promised to redress the wrongs
His ancestors had wrought;
And first expelled from out the court
The Normans Rufus brought.

He then restored the Saxon laws,
And chose a Saxon bride,—
Matilda, great-grand-daughter of
King Edward Ironside.

And he recalled from banishment
Anselm of Canterbury;
(The first archbishop who decreed
That clergy should not marry.)

* Fine scholar. He had heard his father say, that illiterate kings were about like crowned asses, and he was resolved not to be considered as one of these.

Then Robert, England's rightful heir,
Came from the first crusade;
He strove, by force, to gain the crown,
But fruitless efforts made.

Far into Normandy he fled;
But there King Henry hied,
And conquered it, and Robert threw
In prison, where he died.

Then Robert's son he captured, that
His own might wear the crown;
But blasted was his lofty hope,
When the "White Ship"* went down.

Then the first stone-arched bridge was built,
By Queen Matilda's aid;
Then, in eleven thirty-four,
The first canal was made.†

---

* The name of the vessel in which the prince was drowned.

† Queen Matilda built two bridges at Stratford, in Essex (thence called De Arcubus or Le Bow). — *Goldsmith.*

The first canal made in England, was by Henry the First, when the river Trent was joined to the Witham, A. D. 1134. — *Williams.*

CONTEMPORARY SOVEREIGNS.

Popes.	A. D.	Emperors of the East.	A. D.	Kings of France.	A. D.
Pascal II.	1099	Alexis I.	1081	Philip I.	1060
Gelastius II.	1118	John Comnenus	1118	Louis VI.	1108
Calixtus II.	1119				
		Emperors of the West.		Kings of Scotland.	
Honorius II.	1124				
Innocent II.	1130	Henry IV.	1056	Donald VIII.	1068
		Henry V.	1106	Edgar	1108
		Lotharius	1125	Alexander	1117
				David	1124

STEPHEN OF BLOIS.*

1135—1154. 19 YEARS.

Stephen, a nephew of the king,
Usurped the vacant throne;
And passed his reign in contests with
Matilda, and her son.

All England swarmed with fortresses;
Large villages were found
Without an inmate, others lay
In ruins on the ground.

Eleven hundred castles rose,
By feudal chieftains built,
Whose swords, in rival chieftain's blood,
Were dripping to the hilt.†

* A city of France.

† Each chief sided with one or the other party. Those who took

About this time was chivalry*
In England introduced;
And with it came the Tournament,†
The Romance,‡ and the Joust.§

---

the oath of fealty to Stephen, required, as the price of submission, the right of fortifying their castles.

* This was an institution common to Europe from the 10th to the 15th century (the period of the middle or dark ages). It owed its origin to feudalism, and it expired with it. It was designed to correct some of the evils incident to that state of society. The feudal lord exercised an almost unlimited power over his vassals. The knight of chivalry swore to fulfil his duty as the champion of God and the ladies. He devoted himself to speak the truth, to maintain the right, to protect the distressed, to practise courtesy, to fulfil obligations, and to vindicate his honour and character in every perilous adventure.

† Tournaments were martial sports, or exercises, performed by two parties of cavaliers, with inoffensive weapons. The word is derived from *tourner*, to turn round; because great dexterity of both man and horse were required. The arrangements were magnificent and costly, especially when they were designed to celebrate coronations, the marriages of princes, or military victories. Wealth, fashion, and beauty, thronged to these exhibitions; and the successful knight received the reward of his prowess from the hand of some chosen fair one. No knight could tourney who had violated any of the rules of chivalry.

‡ Romances were books which described extravagant chivalric feats; with stories of magicians, dragons, and giants; invulnerable men, winged horses, enchanted armour, and enchanted castles. Among those most celebrated, were "The Seven Champions of Christendom," "Sir Launcelot," "Charlemagne and his Twelve Peers," and "King Arthur and the Knights of the Round Table."

§ The joust was not so favourite an amusement as the tournament,

CONTEMPORARY SOVEREIGNS.

Popes.	A. D.	Emperors of the East.	A. D.	Kings of France.	A. D.
Celestine II.....	1143	John Comnenus	1118	Louis VI.	1108
Lucius II.	1144	Man. Comnenus	1143	Louis VII.	1137
Eugenius III. ...	1145	**Emperors of the West.**		**King of Scotland.**	
Anastasius IV...	1153	Lothaire II.	1125	David I.	1124
Adrian IV......	1154	Conrad III......	1138		
		Frederick I.....	1152		

HOUSE OF PLANTAGENET.*—11 KINGS.

HENRY II.

Reigned from Dec. 8th, 1154, to July 6th, 1189. 34¾ Years.

Henry dismissed the foreign troops
  Called during Stephen's reign,
Destroyed the castles, and restored
  Order and peace again.

---

for baronial pomp was not necessary to its display. It often followed the tournament. The victor knight would ride about the lists, and call on the surrounding cavaliers, by their valiancy, and for their love of the ladies, to encounter him in their strokes of the lance.—*Royal Robbins.*

* Antiquaries are at a loss to account for the origin of this appellation. Some say that Fulk, the first earl of Anjou, of that name, being stung with remorse for some wicked action, went on a pil-

Charters he gave to towns, by which
A citizen could claim
From none, inferior to himself,
The *freeman's* honoured name.*

And "circuit judges" were compelled
Throughout the land to ride,†
That, in the place of feudal chiefs,
They might disputes decide.

Next were the "Constitutions framed
Of Clarendon,"‡ becaus
The clergy were amenable
Not to the "common laws."

Thus were the *people* recognized;
And never, from that hour,

---

grimage to Jerusalem as a work of atonement, where, being scourged with broom-twigs growing on the spot, he took the surname of Plantagenet, or Broom-stalk, which was retained by his posterity. Putnam William, of Malmsbury, says "that the name originated from Geoffry Martel, the young count of Anjou, wearing in his helmet a bunch of flowering broom (*plante-de-genet*), instead of a plume."

* It has been previously mentioned that, in the early days of feudalism, the feudal chief had unlimited power over his retainers. Some of these, who had been freed by the chiefs, had now gone into towns, and engaged in arts and commerce; others had settled upon small estates as independent owners.

† He divided the kingdom into circuits.

‡ Named from the place where they were enacted.

Did king, nor priest, nor feudal chief,
  Regain the former power.

Becket,* the favourite of the king,
  Had regal pomp assumed;
High Chancellor then, Archbishop now,
  Upon his rank presumed,

And steadily opposed the plan
  The people's rights to save;
But he was murdered,—and the king
  Did penance at his grave.

---

* Thomas à Becket was the son of a private soldier, and was the first man of English extraction who had arrived at any eminence in political life since the time of the Norman conquest. As one evidence of his luxurious habits while High Chancellor, his secretary, Fitz-Stephen, tells us "that in winter his apartments were every day covered with clean hay and straw, and in summer, with green rushes, or boughs, that the gentlemen who paid court to him, and who could not by reason of their numbers find a place at table, might not soil their fine clothes by sitting on a dirty floor." This does not seem *to us* to accord very well with the scarlet coat lined with ermine, which he is described as wearing. After he became Archbishop of Canterbury, he assumed the greatest austerity,—ate only bread, drank water, in which fennel had been steeped to make it nauseous, and wore sackcloth next his skin, which he would not change until it became filled with vermin. He was killed at a suggestion of the king, who afterward repented of the act. Becket was canonized; and it is said that, within the space of one year, 150,000 pilgrims resorted to his tomb.

The third of France to Henry came,
  As Eleanora's dower;
No king in Christendom was found
  Possessing so much power.

And by Earl Pembroke's (Strongbow's) aid,
  He gained all Ireland, too,
And unto England 'twas annexed,
  Eleven seventy-two.

In early days had Ireland been
  A refuge for the learned,
'Till the incursions of the Danes,
  When ruder times returned.

From darkness slowly it emerged,
  Though not until the reign
Of Edward First, did England's laws
  Throughout the realm obtain.

The sons of Henry strove to wrest
  The sceptre from his hand,
Joined by the French and Scottish kings,
  And barons of the land.

Transient advances learning made
  In this and Stephen's reign,
For both the monarchs patronized
  Letters and learned men.

Henry of Huntingdon* we find,
William of Malmsbury,†
Cambrensis,‡ and de Hovedon,§
And John of Salisbury;||

And Simeon of Durham,¶ with
Pulleyn,** Glanville,†† St. Victor,‡‡
And Layamon,§§ Nigellus,|||| and
Joseph of Exeter.¶¶

Few of the laity could read;
Authors were priests alone;
But books were multiplied, for now
Had paper become known.***

---

* Chronicles of England.
† Died 1143. History of Britain.
‡ (Geraldus) Conquest of Ireland, &c.
§ (Roger) Chronicles of England.
|| Died 1181. Life of Becket, &c.
¶ Chronicles of England.
** (Robert) died 1150. Theology.
†† (Ralph) collection of laws.
‡‡ (Richard) died 1173. Theology.
§§ Ten Saxon poems.
|||| Speculum stultorum.
¶¶ Trojan War, War of Antioch, Epics.
*** In every monastery was a room called the writing-room, where the younger monks employed themselves in writing manuscripts, for the art of printing was not yet invented.

CONTEMPORARY SOVEREIGNS.

Popes.	A. D.		A. D.	Kings of Portugal.	A. D.
Adrian IV......	1154	Alexis II.......	1180	Alphonso	1102
Alexander III...	1159	Andronicus I....	1183	Sancho I.	1185
Lucius III.	1181	Isaac Angelus ..	1185	**King of Denmark.**	
Urban III.	1185	**Emperor of the West.**		Waldemar	1157
Gregory VIII....	1187	Frederick I.	1152	**Kings of Scotland.**	
Clement III.....	1188	**Kings of France.**		David I.	1124
Emperors of the East.		Louis VII.	1137	Malcolm IV. ...	1153
Man. Comnenus	1143	Philip Augustus.	1180	William	1165

RICHARD I., CŒUR-DE-LION.*

1189—1299.

King Richard sold the royal lands,
And every effort made
Gold to procure, that he might go
Upon the third Crusade.

At Acre, Joppa, Ascalon,
With Saladin he fought;
Small was the gain, yet terrible
The carnage that was wrought.†

---

* Lion-hearted.

† At Acre alone, upwards of 300,000 of the Crusaders were killed.

The truce of three years and three months,
Of three days and three hours,*
Left the sea-ports of Palestine
Alone with Christian powers.

Richard, brave, generous, might have won
A high and lofty fame,
Yet childhood's cheek but blanched with fear
At mention of his name.

Returning in disguise, he was
By Henry captive made;
One hundred fifty thousand marks
Were for his ransom paid.

During his absence, England was
A prey to force and strife;
No law defended property,
And none protected life.

And numerous were the robber hordes;
And then were Robin Hood†
And his companion, Little John,
The terror of the wood.

---

* I have mentioned the length of this truce, because it was so curious. The number three is considered by some Christians to have a peculiar significance.

† Robin Hood, with Little John, his second in command, were the celebrated captains of a notorious band of robbers, who infested the forest of Sherwood, in Nottinghamshire, and from thence made excursions to many parts of England, in search of booty, from 1189 to

CONTEMPORARY SOVEREIGNS.

Popes.	A. D.	Emperors of the West.	A. D.	King of Portugal.	A. D.
Clement III	1188	Frederick I.	1152	Sancho I.	1180
Celestine III.	1191	Henry VI.	1190	**King of Denmark.**	
Innocent III.	1198	Philip I.	1197	Canute V.	1182
Emperors of the East.					
Isaac II.	1186	**King of France.**		**King of Scotland.**	
Alexis III.	1195	Philip II.	1180	William	1165

JOHN LACKLAND.*

Reigned from April 6th, 1199, to October 7th, 1216. 17½ Years.

Philip of France upheld the claim
Of Arthur to the throne,†
And seized upon that half of France
Which England called her own.

John made the pope his enemy,‡
Who used his power to lay

1247. Some historians say that this was only a name assumed by the then earl of Huntingdon, who was disgraced and banished the court by Richard I. at his accession. — *Stowe's Chron.*

* Named from the loss of his French possessions.

† Arthur of Brittany — his nephew.

‡ Innocent III. He offended him by refusing to receive Stephen Langton as Archbishop of Canterbury because the pope had elected him.

1208. The kingdom 'neath an interdict,*
And give his crown away.

He excommunicated him;†
And then did John agree
To hold the throne in vassalage
Unto the Holy See.

But by the barons he was forced
To sign, at Runnimede,
The "Magna Charta,"‡ which to all
Important rights did cede.

---

* When a country is laid under an interdict by the pope, the doors of the churches are closed, the statues of the saints are laid upon the ground, diversions of all kinds are forbidden, marriages are performed in the church-yards, and the dead are denied funeral service, and buried in ditches and holes by the way-side. The whole kingdom was under an interdict for six years.

† When a king is excommunicated, his subjects are absolved from allegiance to him, and he is denounced as unholy and polluted. When Henry IV. of Germany was excommunicated, 1077, his body was five years above ground, no one presuming to bury it.

‡ The Magna Charta (Great Charter) contained sixty-three clauses; an enumeration of some of which may afford an idea of the previous condition of the people. "It was decreed that the goods of every free man shall be disposed of, after his death, according to his will; that if he die without a will, his children shall succeed to his property; that no officer of the crown shall take horses, carts, or wood, without the consent of the owner; that no free man shall be imprisoned, outlawed, or banished, unless by the judgment of his peers, or the laws of the land; that *even* a rustic shall not, by any fine, be deprived of his carts, ploughs, and implements of husbandry. This last was the only article in that great charter for the protection of the labouring people." — *Mrs. Markham.*

A "Charter of the Forest,"* too,
He gave; — but in his ire
Called foreign aid, and wasted wide
His realm with sword and fire.

Degree of Doctor was conferred
Twelve hundred and sixteen;
In London, many houses still
With thatch of straw were seen.†

CONTEMPORARY SOVEREIGNS.

Popes.	A. D.	Emperors of the West.	A. D.	Kings of Portugal.	A. D.
Innocent III.	1198	Philip	1197	Sancho I.	1185
Honorius III.	1215	Otho IV.	1208	Adolphus II.	1212
		Frederick II.	1211		
Emperors of the East.				**King of Denmark.**	
Alexis III.	1195			Waldemar II.	1202
Alexis IV.	1203	**King of France.**			
Alexis V.	1204	Philip II.	1189	**Kings of Scotland.**	
Theodore I.	1205			William	1165
				Alexander II.	1214

* This charter allowed the proprietors of forests to enclose them for their own private purposes, and it abolished the royal privilege of killing game all over the kingdom.

† The houses of the city of London were till this period mostly thatched with *straw;* for it appears that an order was issued that all houses therein should be covered with tiles or slate, instead of straw, more especially such as stood in the best streets. — *Haydn.*

The common language of kings is we, which plural style was begun with King John, A. D. 1199. — *Coke's Instit.* Before this time, sovereigns used the singular in all their edicts. — *Haydn.*

HENRY III.

1216—1272. 56 YEARS.

Henry on foreigners bestowed
  Each office of command,
And by his vain expenditures,
  Impoverished the land.

The barons, to resistance roused,
  By the Earl Leicester led,
Forced from the feeble king a grant
  That they should rule instead.

But seeking in the parliaments*
  The nobles' good alone,
The *people* looked for means whereby
  To make their grievance known.

They formed a new assembly, where
  Twelve from each borough sate,
1253. And from this time we find the House
  Of Commons takes its date.

* The word parliament is derived from *parler-la-ment*, which, in the Norman law style, signifies *to speak one's mind.* — *Barton.*

This name was adopted about the time of the Norman conquest. That which the Saxons gave to an assembly of the wise men of the nation, was *witena-mot*, or witena-gemot.

The king and prince had captive been,
But now the prince set free,
At *Evesham* o'er the barons gained
A signal victory.

The fire and water ordeals* were
Abolished in this reign;
Then was the chimney sometimes seen,
And the glass window-pane.

Then first the table of the rich
The cup and saucer graced;
Then by the tallow-candle was
The torch of wood replaced.

---

* The fire and water ordeals were introduced into England, with other superstitions, taken from the codes of the Germans, about the time of Edward the Confessor. That by fire, was confined to the upper classes of the people; that by water, to the bondsmen and rustics. Hence the expression of going through fire and water to serve another. A prisoner who pleaded "not guilty," might choose whether he would put himself for trial upon God and his country, by twelve men, as at this day, or upon God only; and then it was called the judgment of God, presuming he would deliver the innocent. The accused were to pass barefooted and blindfolded over nine red-hot ploughshares, or were to carry burning irons in their hands; and accordingly as they escaped, they were judged innocent or guilty, acquitted or condemned. The water ordeal was performed in either hot or cold water: in cold water, the parties suspected were adjudged innocent, if their bodies were borne up by the water, contrary to the course of nature; in hot water, they were to put their bare arms or legs into scalding water, which if brought out unhurt, they were adjudged innocent of the crime. — *Haydn.*

1234. And then we find coal first was used,*
And linen then was wrought;
Then the first poet laureate;†
Astronomy then taught.‡

Paris, a Benedictine monk,
The papal power withstood;
Historian, poet, orator,
Learned, and wise, and good.

In this reign Roger Bacon lived,—
To him our thanks are due
For telescopes, for spectacles,
And for glass-mirrors, too.

Then Roger, of Wendover, wrote;
Grosseteste, Holes and Neckham,
Robert of Gloucester, Holywood,
And Kishanger and Peckham.

---

* The first charter for digging coal was granted in 1239.—*Haydn.*

† He was styled "The King's Versifier," and a hundred shillings a year were his annual stipend. — *Maddox.*

‡ But so late as the reign of Edward VI., 1552, books of astronomy and geometry were burned as being infested with magic.

CONTEMPORARY SOVEREIGNS.

Popes.	A. D.
Honorius III.	1216
Gregory IX.	1227
Celestine IV.	1241
Innocent IV.	1243
Alexander IV.	1254
Urban IV.	1261
Clement IV.	1225
Gregory X.	1271

Emperors of the East.	A. D.
Theodore I.	1204
John III.	1922
Theodore II.	1225
John IV.	1259
Michael VIII.	1259

Emperor of the West.	A. D.
Frederick II.	1211

Kings of France.	A. D.
Philip II.	1180
Louis VIII.	1223
St. Louis IX.	1226
Philip III.	1270

Kings of Portugal.	A. D.
Alphonso III.	1202
Sancho II.	1233
Alphonsus V.	1247

Kings of Denmark.	A. D.
Waldemar	1202
Eric VI.	1240
Abel I.	1250
Christopher I.	1252
Eric VIII.	1259

King of Sweden.	A. D.
Waldemar	1250

Kings of Scotland.	A. D.
Alexander II.	1214
Alexander III.	1249

EDWARD I., LONGSHANKS.

1272—1307. 35 YEARS.

Edward invaded Wales, and in
  Twelve hundred eighty-three
Attached the conquered nation to
  The English monarchy.

The queen of Scotland dying now,
  Bruce and Baliol claimed
The vacant throne, — and umpire there
  Edward the latter named.

But Edward strove to rule the land,
  Weakened by civil war;
And entering Scotland, he subdued
  Baliol at *Dunbar*.

Then Wallace, Scotia's hero, sought
  His country's chains to burst,
At *Falkirk* he was captured, though
  Victorious at the first.

Escaped from prison, Bruce arose,
  His native land to free;
And Edward died while planning schemes
  For its captivity.

In England, liberty progressed;
  A signal point was gained;
For funds could be, but by consent
  Of parliament, obtained.

The Magna Charta was confirmed,
1289. And the last tribute paid
Unto the pope; and then the first
1272. Treaty of commerce made.*

---

* The first ever made with a foreign nation is said by some to have been with Norway, but by Anderson to have been with the Flemmings (natives of Flanders).

CONTEMPORARY SOVEREIGNS.

Popes.	A. D.
Gregory X.	1271
Innocent V.	1276
Adrian V.	1276
John XXI.	1276
Nicholas III.	1277
Martin	1281
Honorius IV.	1285
Nicholas IV.	1288
Celestine V.	1294
Boniface VIII.	1294
Benedict IX.	1303
Clement V.	1305

Emperors of the East.	A. D.
Michael VIII.	1259
Andronicus II.	1283
Emperors of the West.	
Frederick II.	1212
Rudolphus I.	1273
Adolphus of Nassau	1291
Albert	1298
Kings of France.	
Philip III.	1270
Philip IV.	1285

Kings of Portugal.	A. D.
Alphonso III.	1247
Dyonisius	1275
Kings of Denmark.	
Eric VII.	1259
Eric VIII.	1286
Kings of Sweden.	
Magnus II.	1279
Berger II.	1299
Kings of Scotland.	
Alexander III.	1246
John Baliol	1293
Robert Bruce	1306

EDWARD II., CAERNARVON.*

Reigned from July 7th, 1307, to Sept. 21st, 1327. 20 Years.

Edward was weak, and wholly ruled
By favourites, vicious, mean,
Hence strife and civil wars ensued,
Led by the earls and queen.

Determined to preserve his crown,
Again The Bruce arose,
At *Bannockburn* he met the king,
And triumphed o'er his foes.

* So called from the place of his birth. He had been crowned by the Scots just before the death of Edward I.

And thus was he securely placed
  Upon the Scottish throne,
But since the Conquest, such defeat
  Had England never known.

Edward deposed, imprisoned, was
  Killed by his queen's command;
The courts were closed, disorder reigned
  Uncurbed throughout the land.*

CONTEMPORARY SOVEREIGNS.

Popes.	A. D.		A. D.	Kings of Denmark.	A. D.
Clement V.	1305	Henry VIII.	1304	Eric VIII.	1286
John XXII.	1316	Lewis IV.	1314	Christopher II.	1319
		Kings of France.			
Emperors of the East.		Philip IV.	1289	**Kings of Sweden.**	
Andronicus II.	1283	Lewis X.	1314	Berger II.	1290
Andronicus III.	1320	Philip V.	1316	Magnus III.	1320
		Charles IV.	1322		
Emperors of the West.		**Kings of Portugal.**		**King of Scotland.**	
Albert I.	1298	Dyonisius	1272	Robert Bruce	1306
		Alphonso IV.	1325		

* In consequence of war, agriculture was neglected; and because of this, the labouring classes suffered for want of food. The nobles lived wastefully, and Edward strove to check their extravagance by a royal proclamation, which is interesting, as it shows the control the king exercised over the private affairs of his subjects. They were forbidden to have more than two courses at dinner, for, "by the outrageous and excessive multitude of meats and dishes which the great men of our kingdom have used, and still use in their castles, many great evils have come upon our kingdom, the health of our

EDWARD III.

1327—1377. 50 YEARS.

"Heroic" has this reign been called,
  Its conquests "brilliant," "great,"
Its wars were most *unjust*, and brought
  But *evil* to the state.

With wisdom Edward might have ruled,—
  He was accomplished, learned;
But with his son, the famed Black Prince,
  His thoughts on *conquest* turned.

Twice did they triumph o'er the Scotch,*
  And with the French† they waged

---

subjects has been injured, their goods consumed," &c. There were at that time very few culinary vegetables in general use, excepting carrots, parsnips, and cabbages. Potatoes were not introduced until the reign of Elizabeth.

Richard II. entertained every day two thousand persons at his table. The Normans were in ancient times distinguished from the Saxons by their abstemiousness, but now they were guilty of the greatest extravagance. At the marriage banquet of Richard, earl of Cornwall, in 1243, thirty thousand dishes were served up. Although there were but two meals in the day, the greater part of it was occupied in eating them.

* Under Robert Bruce, and afterwards under his son David.

† Edward's mother had three brothers, who were successively kings of France, but who all died leaving only daughters. The Salic law prevailed in France, excluding women from inheriting the crown, and Edward claimed that it belonged to him.

A war, which more than twenty years
  With blinding fury raged.

At *Cressy*, *Poictiers*, and *Calais*,*
  Though victories were gained,
E'er Edward's death, Calais was all
  That unto him remained.

Weaving of cloth was introduced †
  In thirteen thirty-one;
Then first to patents was affixed
  The broad seal of the crown.

The Windsor Castle was rebuilt,‡
  Each county sent its men;
The laws had been in French before,§
  They were in English then.

---

* These victories were chiefly won by archers.—*Northrop's History of London.*

† By two weavers from Brabant, who settled at York.

‡ Edward's method of conducting the work may serve as a specimen of the condition of the people in that age. No contracts were made with workmen, as in the present times, but every county in England was assessed to send the king a certain number of masons, tilers, and carpenters, who were to perform their quota of labour. —*R. Robbins.*

§ Since the period of the Conquest.

Then jester,* fool,† and juggler,‡ gave
To king and court delight,
And chivalry about that time
Attained its greatest height.

Then the first English traveller
Of any note we find,
The learned Sir John Mandeville,
Accomplished and refined.

CONTEMPORARY SOVEREIGNS.

Popes.	A. D.	Emperors of the West.	A. D.	Kings of Denmark.	A. D.
John XXII.	1316	Louis IV.	1314	Christopher II.	1319
Benedict XI.	1334	Charles IV.	1347	Waldemar III.	1340
Clement VI.	1342			Olaus III.	1375
Innocent VI.	1352	**Kings of France.**		**Kings of Sweden.**	
Urban V.	1362	Charles IV.	1322	Magnus III.	1320
Gregory XI.	1370	Philip VI.	1328	Albert.	1363
		John I.	1353		
Emperors of the East.		Charles V.	1364	**Kings of Scotland.**	
Andronicus III.	1320			Robert Bruce	1306
John V.	1341	**Kings of Portugal.**		David II.	1330
John VI.	1355	Alphonsus IV.	1325	Edward Baliol	1332
		Pedro I.	1357	David II. (restor.)	1342
		Ferdinand I.	1367	Robert (Stuart)	1370

* In some ancient works a jester is described as a witty and jocose person, kept by princes to inform them of their faults, and of those of other men, under the disguise of a waggish story. Many of the English kings kept jesters and fools. There was a jester at court in the reign of James I., but we hear of no licensed jester afterwards.

† The dress of the fool was of many colours, and ornamented with little sheep-bells, which, like bells of the old women in the nursery-song, made music wherever he went.

‡ Jugglers were a class of itinerant players, who played and per-

RICHARD II.

1377—1399. 22 YEARS.

The duke of Gloucester,* duke of York,
  And the famed John of Gaunt,
With private feuds and public wars
  Reduced the land to want.

A "poll-tax," levied on each one
  O'er fifteen years of age,
Was brutally enforced, and then
  Burst forth the people's rage.

By long oppression goaded on,
  They rose in arms to claim,
(Led by Wat Tyler and Jack Shaw,)
  The freeman's rights and name.†

Charters were given, but annulled
  When quiet was restored,
And each returned to villanage‡
  Under his feudal lord.

---

formed ridiculous feats in the king's palace and noblemen's hall, for the entertainment of their guests. They were sometimes elevated upon carts in the public streets, that the poorer people might have the benefit of their exhibitions.

* Pronounced Gloss′ter.

† When asked by the king what they wanted, they replied, "The freedom of ourselves and our children."

‡ The slaves held under the feudal system were called "villains."

King Richard seized on lands to which
Hereford* was rightful heir;
But while away in Ireland,
Quelling disturbance there,

Hereford returned from banishment,
Gathered his friends around,
And Richard was deposed, and he
As 'Henry Fourth'' was crowned.

Chaucer and Gower, often styled
"Fathers of English song,"
And Wickliffe, the reformer bold,†
Unto this time belong.

CONTEMPORARY SOVEREIGNS.

Popes.	A. D.	Kings of France.	A. D.	Queen of Sweden.	A. D.
Gregory XI.	1370	Charles V.	1364	Margaret held Sweden with Denmark	1397
Urban VI.	1378	Charles VI.	1380		
Boniface IX.	1389				
Emperors of the East.		**Kings of Portugal.**		**Kings of Scotland.**	
John VI.	1355	Ferdinand	1367	Robert II.	1370
Emanuel II.	1391	John I.	1385	Robert III.	1390
Emperors of the West.		**King and Queen of Denmark.**			
Charles IV.	1347	Olaus III.	1375		
Winceslaus	1378	Margaret	1385		

* Henry, earl of Hereford, was the oldest son and heir of John of Gaunt, duke of Lancaster.

† Professor of divinity in the University of Oxford. He was called the morning star of the Reformation. He was the first who opposed the authority of the pope, the jurisdiction of the bishops, and the temporalities of the church. — *Mortimer.*

BRANCH OF LANCASTER. — 3 KINGS.

1399—1461. 60 YEARS.

HENRY IV., BOLINGBROKE.

1399—1413. 14 YEARS.

When Henry gained the throne, to which
He had no rightful claim,*
Scarce one conspiracy was crushed
Before another came.

Northumberland the English led;
The Scotch and Welsh arose;
At *Shrewsbury* they met the king,
Who triumphed o'er his foes.

There Douglas fought and Percy fell —
Heroes renowned in story —
But round their heads a halo rests,
Simply of martial glory.

The people still resolved to place
The crown on Edward's head,

* After the deposition of Richard, Edmund Mortimer was the true heir.

1405. And Henry quelled another force,
By York's Archbishop led.*

Victor at length, he strove to please
The people more and more,
And to the House of Commons gave
A power unknown before.

Then first the persecution of
The Wickliffites began;
He was the first of England's kings
Who gave his brother man

To scaffold or to flame, if found
To hold another creed
From that which he thought right, or deemed
Sufficient for his need.

And he detained the Scottish prince,
(James First,) a captive long,
But the dark prison hours he soothed
With music† and with song.

These songs have come to us, and place
James First of Scotland's name
Among the lyrists of the time,
High on the scroll of fame.

---

* Scroop. He was beheaded, and this was the first time in England that the penalty of death was inflicted upon a *bishop*.

† He is said to have been the first who reduced the wild, sweet melody of Scotland to the rules of composition.

CONTEMPORARY SOVEREIGNS.

Popes.	A. D.	Emperors of the West.	A. D.	King and Queen of Denmark and Sweden.	A. D.
Boniface IX.	1389	Winceslaus	1378	Margaret	1385
Innocent VII.	1404	Robert Le Pet	1400	Eric XIII.	1411
Gregory XII.	1406	Sigismund	1410		
Alexander V.	1409	King of France.		King of Scotland.	
John XXIII.	1410	Charles VI.	1380	Robert III.	1390
Emperor of the East.		King of Portugal.			
Emanuel II.	1391	John I.	1385		

HENRY V.

1413—1422. 9 YEARS.

Henry maintained the claim to France
By bold and desperate war,
And gained a bloody victory on
The field of *Agincourt:*

Look Normandy and part of France,
Married its princess there,
Was regent of the realm proclaimed,
And to its throne the heir.*

* About this time, to the dark, grim stone castle of the feudal days, succeeded the brighter and more hospitable-looking mansion, built of timber, plastered without, and richly carved within. On

CONTEMPORARY SOVEREIGNS.

Popes. A. D.	Emperor of the West. A. D.	King of Denmark and Sweden. A. D.
John XXIII. 1410	Sigismund 1410	Eric XIII....... 1411
Martin V....... 1417		
Emperor of the East.	**King of France.**	**King of Scotland.**
Emanuel II..... 1394	Charles VI. 1380	Robert III..... .1390
	King of Portugal.	
	John I. 1385	

HENRY VI.

1422—1461. 39 YEARS.

Henry, of England and of France
The monarch was proclaimed,
And Gloucester's duke and Bedford's duke
His guardians were named.

---

an elevated portion, (called the *dais*,) in the large and scantily-furnished hall, the host feasted his numerous guests. The dancers danced, the minstrel played, the jester told his story, and the juggler performed his feats for their entertainment. Above them perched the hawks; below them, the dogs quarrelled for the bones which were thrown them; the servants shouted and screamed in their boisterous merriment, and after devouring their portion of the feast, carried the remainder to the poor, who, in eager expectation, crowded around the gates to receive it.

Had England conquered Orleans, then
  All France had been her own,
But she was forced to raise the siege
  By the intrepid Joan.

Thus "Joan of Arc"* her country saved;
  And at no distant day,
England lost all she owned in France,
  Save Guienne and Calais.

Joan crowned the king at Rheims; but when
  The chance of battle turned,
She fell among the English, and
  For witchcraft she was burned.†

Now Richard, duke of York, arose
  To claim the English throne;
The "wars of York and Lancaster"‡
  Sprang from this cause alone.

Joan of Arc was a servant in Neufchatel, in Lorraine. She imagined herself delegated by God to raise the siege of Orleans, and to restore to Charles the kingdom of his ancestors. She was taken at the siege of Compigne by the English, and burnt for a witch, in the 29th year of her age.

† Charles, whom she had just crowned, made no effort to save her. The French soldiers were jealous of her; and when a party which she headed were repulsed, near Compigne, and retreated into the town, the governor shut her out, and she fell into the hands of the English.

‡ These wars were also styled "The Wars of the Two Roses." The white rose was the symbol of the house of York; the red, of

From Lionel, the second son
  Of Edward Third, he came;
From the third son of Edward Third
  Was the sixth Henry's claim.

In fourteen hundred fifty-five
  Was the first battle fought;
'Twas at St. Albans, and the duke
  Of York the conquest wrought.

The king was captured, but his queen
  The bloody strife maintained;
At *Wakefield*, o'er the duke of York,
  The victory she gained.

He died; but Edward, his young son,
  Was the next victor named;
Then entering London, amid shouts
  He was the king proclaimed.

The house of Lancaster, to keep
  Possession of the throne,
Conferred on parliament a power
  Before that time unknown.

---

that of Lancaster. It seems like desecrating these beautiful flowers to connect them, even in *thought*, with anything so sanguinary and God-defying as war!

CONTEMPORARY SOVEREIGNS.

Popes.	A. D.
Martin V.	1417
Eugenius IV.	1431
Nicholas V.	1447
Calixtus III.	1455
Pius II.	1458
Emperors of the West.	
Sigismund	1410
Albert II.	1438
Frederick III.	1440
Emperors of the East.	
Emanuel II.	1391
John VII.	1429
Constantine III., and last Christian emperor, succeeded by his conqueror, Mahomet II., who took Constantinople by storm, May 29,	1453
Kings of France.	
Charles VII.	1452
Louis XI.	1461
Kings of Portugal.	
John I.	1385
Edward	1433
Alphonsus V.	1438
Kings of Scotland.	
Robert III.	1390
James I.	1424
James II.	1437
James III.	1460
Kings of Denmark and Sweden.	
Eric IX.	1411
Christopher III.	1439
Christian I.	1448

HOUSE OF YORK.—3 KINGS.

EDWARD IV.

Reigned from March 5th, 1461, to April 9th, 1483. 22 Years.

Yet still was Edward insecure
  Upon tho Engliсh throne;
The *Towton* battle he had gained
  In fourteen sixty-one.

And more than forty thousand men
 Fell on the field that day,
And they were *husbands, fathers, sons,*
 That dead and dying lay.

The war of the twin roses still
 Raged wildly in this reign—
The Lancasterians would now,
 And now the Yorkists gain.

But Margaret, for the infant prince,
 Urged the fierce battles on,
Until at Tewkesbury subdued,
 In fourteen seventy-one.

Henry was murdered, the young prince
 Slain by the noble's lance,
The captive Margaret ransomed by
 Louis, the king of France.

And thus the bloody contest closed,
 Which had for sixteen years
Deluged the land with human blood,
 And watered it with tears.

But an achievement worthier note
 In seventy-one was wrought,
For Caxton into England then
 The art of printing brought.*

* To the west of the sanctuary in Westminster Abbey stood the Eleemosynary or Almonry, where the first printing-press in England

About this time the fisheries
  First into notice came;
Commerce extended, opening thus
  The surest road to fame.*

CONTEMPORARY SOVEREIGNS.

Popes. A. D.	Emperors of the Turks. A. D.	Kings of Denmark and Sweden. A. D.
Pius II......... 1458	Mahomet II..... 1453	Christian I...... 1448
Paul II......... 1464	Bajazet II. 1481	John I. 1481
Sextus IV. 1471		
Emperor of Germany.	**King of France.**	**King of Scotland.**
Frederick III. .. 1440	Louis XI. 1461	James III. 1460
	Kings of Portugal.	
	Alphonsus V.... 1438	
	John II. 1481	

---

was erected, in 1471, by William Caxton, encouraged by the learned Thomas Milling, then abbot. He published "The Game and Play of the Chesse," the first book ever printed in Great Britain. The title was, "The Game and Play of the Chesse. Translated out of the Frenche, and emprynted by me, William Caxton, Fynysshire, the last day of Marche, the yer of our Lord God a thousand four hundred and lxxiiij."—*Leigh.*

* From 1462 until the present reign, a ridiculous fashion for dressing the feet prevailed among the people. The points of the shoes were so long, that, when walking, the wearers were obliged to tie them to their knees. Some were tied with laces, but the most wealthy gentlemen used silver chains.

7

EDWARD V.

1483—1483. 3 MONTHS.

Young Edward and his brother were
Both smothered in their bed
By Richard, Gloucester's duke, who aimed
To fill the throne instead.

CONTEMPORARY SOVEREIGNS.

Pope.	A. D.	Emperor of the Turks.	A. D.	King of Denmark and Sweden.	A. D.
Sextus IV.	1471	Bajazet II.	1481	John	1481
Emperor of Germany.		**King of France.**		**King of Scotland.**	
Frederick III.	1440	Charles VIII.	1483	James III.	1460
		King of Portugal.			
		John II.	1481		

RICHARD III.

1483—1485. 2 YEARS.

When Gloucester's duke, as Richard Third,
Was king of England known,
Then Henry Tudor, Richmond's earl,
Strove to obtain the throne.

The Welsh around the Tudor thronged,
  And upon *Bosworth* field,
In fourteen hundred eighty-five,
  The king was forced to yield.

Unhonoured and unloved, he fell
  Amid the desperate fray:
The wars of York and Lancaster
  Were ended from that day.

He was the last Plantagenet
  Who sat upon the throne,
Which, for three hundred thirty years,
  Was filled by them alone.

For thirty years these civil wars
  Had ravaged wide the land,
Producing, as war *always must*,
  Crime upon every hand.

One hundred eighty thousand men
  Had fallen in the strife—
One hundred eighty thousand men
  By men deprived of life.

And for the trade of killing men,
  All else had been resigned;
Commerce and letters, and the arts,
  Had everywhere declined.

CONTEMPORARY SOVEREIGNS.

Popes. A. D.	Emperor of the Turks. A. D.	King of Denmark and Sweden. A. D.
Sextus IV. 1471	Bajazet II. 1481	John 1481
Innocent VIII. . . 1484		
Emperor of Germany.	**King of France.**	**King of Scotland.**
Frederick II. . . . 1440	Charles VIII. . . . 1483	James III. 1460
	King of Portugal.	
	John II. 1481	

HOUSE OF TUDOR.—5 KINGS.

HENRY VII.

1485—1509. 24 YEARS.

In Henry Seventh's marriage, were
The houses both combined;*
But hatred unto that of York
Was rooted in his mind.

And from the mass two men arose
In kingly rivalry:
A Perkin Warbeck,† who professed
The duke of York to be;

* He married a princess of the house of York.

† Said to be the son of a converted Jew. He was elegant in his manners, and strongly resembled the Plantagenets. James IV. of Scotland married him to Lady Catherine Douglas, one of the most accomplished women of Scotland.

And Lambert Simnel,* who assumed
  The earl of Warwick's name.
Some of the nobles urged the one,
  And some the other claim.

Warbeck, surrounded by a force
  The Scottish king supplied,
Met Henry's troops, but was subdued,
  And, for his treason, died.

Yet still cabals were multiplied;
  Still insurrections rose;
But Henry, at the last, obtained
  A triumph o'er his foes.

Although his fault was avarice,†
  His reign with good was rife;
He to a warlike people taught
  The useful arts of life:

Commerce and industry sustained—
  Varied improvements planned;

* The son of a baker. He was pardoned, and made a scullion in the king's kitchen.

† Avarice prompted him to oppressive exactions. He is said to have left, at his death, a sum of money, which would be equal, at the present time, to £10,000,000. Still he taught the people frugality, and, by precept and example, the equitable payment of debts.

And John Cabot* equipped, who then
Discovered Newfoundland.†

And he curtailed the nobles' claim—
He raised the mass of men—
And feudalism, tottering long,
Received its death-blow then.‡

---

* A merchant of Venice. Henry furnished him with a fleet of ships.

† He named it *Prima vista* (first seen).

‡ Every town had been built in the neighbourhood of some great castle; partly that the soldiers, always kept there ready armed, might protect the inhabitants from the robbers who lurked in the woods by day, and haunted the open country by night; and partly because there dwelt the wealthiest of the land—the largest consumers of their produce. Henry restored law and order, and encouraged the people to build in situations which presented greater opportunities for commerce, to which he endeavoured to direct their attention.

He lessened the strictness of entail; and this enabled the nobles to sell their estates, many of which were purchased by wealthy commoners. Others received rent for their lands and cottages, in place of military service, and thus from villains the people became tenants,—from being merely followers of their lords to battle, idle dependents upon them in time of peace, they became independent, industrious citizens, and useful subjects. The army was now paid by the government. Thus, by various means, were the privileges of the nobles restricted, the people elevated, and feudalism abolished.

CONTEMPORARY SOVEREIGNS.

Popes.	A. D.
Innocent VIII. . .	1484
Alexander VI. . .	1492
Pius III.	1503
Julius III.	1503

Emperors of Germany.	
Frederick II. . . .	1440
Maximilian I. . .	1493

Emperor of the Turks.	A. D.
Bajazet II.	1481

Kings of France.	
Charles VIII. . . .	1483
Louis XII.	1498

King and Queen of Spain.	
Ferdinand the Catholic and Isabella	1475

Kings of Portugal.	A. D.
John II.	1481
Emanuel	1495

King of Denmark and Sweden.	
John	1481

Kings of Scotland.	
James III.	1460
James IV.	1489

HENRY VIII.

1509—1547. 38 YEARS.

Henry unto his father's throne
With fairest prospects came;
The land at peace, the treasury full,
And none to doubt his claim.

But quickly he invaded France,
And soon, on "*Flodden field*,"
His general, earl of Surrey, forced
The Scottish James to yield.

He took part in the frequent wars
Of Germany and France,

And wasted treasure in the show
Of tournament and lance.*

Capricious and tyrannical,
His minister or wife†
One moment high in favour was,
The next, deprived of life.

The pope opposing a divorce,
He claimed *himself* to be
Head of the Church, and set at naught
The pope's supremacy.

Defending now the ancient faith,
Upholding now the new,
He burned those who, on either side,
Pronounced his faith untrue.

---

* A celebrated meeting occurred between Henry VIII. and Francis I. of France near Calais, June, 1520. The nobility of both kingdoms displayed their magnificence with such emulation and profuse expense, as procured for the place of interview (an open plain) the name of "The Field of the Cloth of Gold." Twenty-eight hundred tents were pitched, mostly covered with silk or cloth of gold. "Many of the nobility involved themselves in heavy debts, and were unable, by the penury of the rest of their lives, to repair the vain splendor of a few days." — *Haydn.* Upon this occasion, Francis addressed Henry as "Your Majesty," which was the first time the title was applied to an English sovereign. It originated among the Romans. James I. coupled it with "Sacred" and "Most Excellent."

† This tyrant had six wives. He divorced two, caused two to be executed, one died, and the last survived him.

The monasteries he dissolved—
  Their revenues he seized—
And he beheaded those who dared
  Deny his right to these.

Because of this, Sir Thomas More,
  And Earl of Surrey died;
Though, famed in letters, they had long
  Been England's joy and pride.

Wolsey, the minister and priest,
  For arts and letters known,
Opposing Henry's will, was from
  His lofty station thrown.

Henry, unawed by parliament,
  Imposed a grievous tax;
But the roused nation summoned him
  To answer for his acts.

The art of painting, at this time,
  He into notice brought;
Holbein he patronised, and called
  Titian unto his court.

In this reign Hampton Court* was built;
  The spinning-wheel first used;

* Hampton Court was built by Cardinal Wolsey, and presented by him, in 1526, to King Henry.

And the first map of England drawn;
  And hats first introduced.*

Then was the first compulsory law,†
  The suffering poor to aid,
And first in fifteen forty-six
  Was legal interest paid.‡

And then, suspended from the waist,
  The looking-glass was seen;§
Then were pins introduced,|| and used
  By Catherine, the queen.

---

* Hats were first manufactured in England by the Spaniards, in 1510; before that time, both men and women wore close, knit, woollen caps. — *Stowe.*

† When the monasteries were dissolved, vast numbers of poor, who had been in the practice of receiving their daily food at the gates, were thrown abroad upon the world, unfed and uncared for, and this produced the immediate necessity for a tax for their maintenance.

‡ It was fixed at 10 per cent. per annum.

§ These were at first very small, and either carried in the pockets of the ladies, or suspended from their girdles.

|| They were made of brass wire, and were brought from France in 1540. They were first used in England, it is said, by Catherine Howard, queen of Henry VIII. Before the invention of pins, both sexes used ribands, loop-holes, laces, with points and tags, clasps, hooks and eyes, and skewers of brass, silver, and gold. They were made in England in 1543. — *Stowe.*

CONTEMPORARY SOVEREIGNS.

Popes.	A. D.	Kings of France.	A. D.	Kings of Denmark. (*Alone.*)	A. D.
Julius II.	1503	Louis XII.	1498	Frederick I.	1524
Leo X.	1513	Francis I.	1515	Christian III.	1534
Adrian VI.	1522	**Kings and Queen of Spain.**		**King of Sweden.** (*Alone.*)	
Clement VII.	1523	Philip I.	1504	Gustavus Vasa	1522
Paul III.	1534	Joan	1506	**Kings and Queen of Scotland.**	
Emperors of Germany.		Charles I.	1516	James IV.	1489
Maximilian I.	1493	**Kings of Portugal.**		James V.	1514
Charles V.	1516	Emanuel	1495	Mary	1542
Emperors of the Turks.		John III.	1521		
Bajazet II.	1481	**Kings of Denmark and Sweden.**			
Selim I.	1512	John	1481		
Soliman II.	1520	Christian II.	1513		

EDWARD VI.

1547—1553. 6 YEARS.

In the short reign of Edward Sixth
  The new religion gained
Many adherents in the land,
  Though blood its garments stained.

It was advanced by Somerset's,
  But most by Cranmer's aid;

Cranmer prepared the creed from which
  The present creed is made.*

The dwellings of that day had floors
  Composed of clay alone,
But in the mansions of the rich
  They were with rushes strown.

And in those halls of luxury
  Were chimneys also found,
While the more common people built
  Their fires upon the ground.

Edward, despite his sister's claims,
  Had signed his crown away,
Urged by Northumberland's bold duke,
  To Jane, the Lady Grey.†

Jane, simple, truthful, learned, and wise,
  Sought not an earthly throne;
Her higher aim had been to wear
  The Christian's crown alone.

---

* He drew up forty-two articles, from which, with some alterations, the present *Thirty-nine Articles* which form the Liturgy of the Episcopal church were formed. They were approved and confirmed by parliament, 1547–8.

† Grand-daughter to a sister of Henry VIII. She was versed in Latin, Hebrew, Chaldee, Arabic, French, and Italian. Fuller says, "She had the innocency of childhood, the beauty of youth, the solidity of middle, the gravity of old age, and all at eighteen!"

CONTEMPORARY SOVEREIGNS.

Popes.	Emperor of the Turks.	King of Denmark.
A. D.	A. D.	A. D.
Paul III........ 1534	Soliman II...... 1520	Christian III.... 1534
Julius III....... 1550		
	King of France.	King of Sweden.
Emperor of Germany and King of Spain.	Henry II........ 1547	Gustavus Vasa.. 1522
Charles V...... 1516	King of Portugal.	Queen of Scotland.
	John III........ 1521	Mary 1542

MARY.

1553—1558. 5 YEARS.

Lady Jane Grey, by wily men
  Forced to ascend the throne,
Filled it ten days, when Mary came
  And claimed it as her own.

Jane and her youthful husband died
  By Mary's stern command,
Who, maddened with a bigot zeal,
  Ruled tyrant in the land.

She brought the English church again
  Within the papal see;
More than three hundred protestants
  She burned for heresy.

Cranmer and Latimer were burned,
Ridley and Rogers, too;
But the *spirit* of the rising faith
No power could e'er subdue.*

Forced by her husband, king of Spain,
Into a foreign war,
She lost Calais, held by the crown
Two hundred years and more.

Then drinking-cups of glass were made;
Then needles† brought from Spain;
But little did the arts advance
In Mary's troubled reign.

---

* It has been estimated that, in addition to those who suffered from imprisonment, fines, and confiscation, two hundred and seventy-seven persons were burned to death. Among these, were forty-five women and four children.

† They were considered of more value than silver. "The first that were made in England were fabricated in Cheapside, London, in the time of Mary, by a negro from Spain; but, as he would not impart the secret, it was lost at his death, and not recovered again till 1566, in the reign of Elizabeth, when Elias Growse, a German, taught the art to the English, who have since brought it to the highest degree of perfection." — *Stowe.*

CONTEMPORARY SOVEREIGNS.

Popes.	A. D.	King of France.	A. D.	King of Denmark.	A. D.
Julius III.	1550	Henry II.	1547	Frederick II.	1549
Marcellus III.	1555				
Paul IV.	1555	**King of Spain.**		**King of Sweden.**	
Emperor of Germany.		Philip II.	1555	Gustavus Vasa.	1522
Charles V.	1519				
Emperor of the Turks.		**King of Portugal.**		**Queen of Scotland.**	
Soliman II.	1520	John III.	1521	Mary	1542

ELIZABETH.

1558—1603. 45 YEARS.

"Our good Queen Bess," the English say,
Hers was a glorious age!
In England's annals never yet
Had been so bright a page.

There Shakspeare, the great dramatist,
Spenser, the poet, shine;
And Bacon, the philosopher,
And Hooker, the divine;

There Hawkins,* Drake,* and Frobisher,*
There Walsingham† and Burleigh,†

* Distinguished navigators. † Distinguished statesmen.

Ben Jonson,* Fletcher,* and Beaumont,*
  Sidney† and Walter Raleigh.‡

Then agriculture, commerce, arts,
  And legislation, gained
Greater importance in the land
  Than they had yet attained.

Then first in India were formed
  Establishments for trade;
Of the East India Company
  These the foundation laid.

At this time England's exports were
  Confined to wool alone;
Then knives were made;§ brick buildings then
  Replaced the wood and stone.||

Then clocks and watches first were seen;**
  Post-offices first used;
First paper-mill and first coach built;††
  Potatoes introduced.

---

* Poets and dramatists. † An accomplished officer and author.

‡ A man illustrious in arms and literature. He was called "the soldier, the sailor, the scholar, the philosopher, the poet, the orator, the historian, the courtier." § 1560.

|| 1598. Elizabeth decreed that the city should not go beyond three miles of the city gates, and that there should be no more than one family in a house. ** Introduced from Germany.

†† They were first called Whirlicotes. A bill was introduced into parliament to prevent *men* from riding in coaches, because it was considered too effeminate.

Then choc'late, and tobacco, too,
  Fans and false hair, were bought;
The coin reduced to standard weight,
  And spoons of silver wrought.

Elizabeth the *villains** freed
  In all the western land,
Speeding the day when no *white* slave
  On England's soil should stand.

But at this very time their trade
  In negro slaves began;
From Africa they stole and sold
  Their helpless fellow man.†

The Protestant religion was
  Established in this reign;
The "Church of England" took the form
  That it doth still retain.‡

The "Invincible Armada," though
  It caused alarm at first,

---

* Slaves.

† Captain, afterwards Sir John Hawkins, has the unenviable fame of being the first Englishman, after the discovery of America, who made a traffic of the human species. — *Haydn.*

‡ 1562. There were forty-two articles in the creed prepared in the reign of Edward VI.; they were now reduced to the present thirty-nine. A further revision took place in 1571, but no important alterations were made.

By England's admirals was met,
  And conquered and dispersed.*

It was the largest armament
  That Europe yet had seen;
'Twas sent by Spain to crush the church,
  And to subdue the queen.

Elizabeth has fixed a stain
  Eternal on her name:
Jealous of Mary, queen of Scots,
  Her beauty and her fame,

And fearful that unto the throne
  Her rival might succeed,
For years she kept her prisoner,
  And then her death decreed.

The Irish conquest, which commenced
  Four hundred years before,
By Mountjoy was completed, when
  This reign was nearly o'er.

The peace of England was preserved,
  With all around at war,
And, as a nation, it became
  Respected near and far.

---

* A storm, which drove many of the Spanish ships on the coast of Zealand, completed the discomfiture.

CONTEMPORARY SOVEREIGNS.

Popes.	A. D.
Paul IV.	1555
Pius IV.	1559
Pius V.	1565
Gregory XIII.	1572
Sextus V.	1585
Urban VII.	1590
Gregory XIV.	1590
Innocent IX.	1591
Clement VIII.	1592
Emperors of Germany.	
Ferdinand I.	1558
Maximilian II.	1564
Rodolphus II.	1576
Emperors of the Turks.	A. D.
Soliman II.	1520
Selim II.	1566
Amurath III.	1574
Mahomet III.	1595
Kings of France.	
Henry II.	1547
Francis II.	1559
Charles IX.	1560
Henry III.	1574
Henry IV.	1589
King of Spain.	
Philip II.	1555
Kings of Portugal.	
Sebastian	1557
Henry	1579
Union of Spain and Portugal.	A. D.
Philip II.	1580
Philip III.	1597
Kings of Denmark.	
Christian IV.	1558
Frederick II.	1559
Kings of Sweden.	
Eric X.	1556
John III.	1569
Sigismund	1592
Queen and King of Scotland.	
Mary	1542
James VI.	1567

STUART FAMILY.—6 KINGS.

JAMES I.

1603—1625. 22 YEARS.

James Sixth of Scotland, Mary's son,
  Elizabeth had named
To fill the throne of England, too,
  And he was king proclaimed.

Raleigh, suspected of a plan
  Upon the hrone to place
Young Arabella Stuart,* who
  Was of the royal race,

Was long imprisoned, then reprieved,
  And after years passed by,
On insufficient evidence,
  He was condemned to die.

James and his parliament were found
  Supporting the new faith,
And the "Gunpowder Plot" was formed
  For putting them to death.

For then 'twas hoped the church of Rome
  Again might bear the rule;
Catesby and Percy formed the plot,
  And Guy Fawkes was their tool.

In Mary's reign the Puritans
  First into notice grew;
In the old world oppressed, they sought
  A refuge in the new.

Their wrongs, the controversies, too,
  In which they bore a part,
Sowed the rich seeds of liberty
  Deep in the nation's heart.

---

* Great-grand-daughter of Henry VII., and, after Mary, queen of Scots, the nearest heir to the throne.

The people had awakened now,
And questioned if there be
A Right Divine* in kings to claim
Undoubted sovereignty.

The king sought funds from parliament,
His favourites to please;
For every sum bestowed, it claimed
Redress of grievances.

As wars were few, taxes were few,
Soldiers were idle men,
And farmers richer than the earls
Of Henry Seventh's reign.

The Bible was translated then,
As 'tis at present used;
Then first the Roman characters
In printing introduced.

Newspapers were established first
In sixteen sixty-two;†

---

* The divine right of kings to rule, and the passive obedience of subjects, was a favourite and warmly-contested doctrine of the Stuarts.

† Mr. Watts, of the British Museum, (1850,) says that the first English paper was the "Weekley Newes," published by Nathaniel Butler in 1662.

A paper was circulated in the reign of Elizabeth; but it was merely to convey the intelligence of the defeat of the Spanish

A school to teach anatomy
From Hunt's exertions grew.

The circulation of the blood
Was then by Harvey shown;
The power of electricity
By Gilbert was made known.

The art of dyeing woollen cloth
From Holland introduced;
Thermometers* and compass† made,
And table-fork first used.

James greater good for Ireland wrought,
In the short time he reigned,
Than England had accomplished, since
The country was obtained.

Armada. The full title was, — "No. 50. *The English Mercurie*, published by authoritie, for the prevention of false reports, imprinted by Christopher Barker, her Highness' printer, No. 50. A journall of what passed since the 21st of this month between her Majestie's fleet and that of Spayne, transmitted by the Lord Highe Admirale to the Lordes of Council." — *World's Progress*.

* Invented, 1608, by William Barlowe.

† Invented, 1620, by Drebel.

CONTEMPORARY SOVEREIGNS.

Popes.	A. D.
Clement VIII.	1592
Leo XI.	1605
Paul V.	1605
Gregory XV.	1621
Urban VIII.	1623

Emperors of Germany.	
Rodolphus II.	1576
Matthias I.	1612
Ferdinand II.	1619

Emperors of the Turks.	A. D.
Achmet I.	1603
Mustapha I.	1617
Osman	1618
Mustapha I. res.	1622
Amurath IV.	1623

Kings of France.	
Henry IV.	1589
Louis XIII.	1610

Kings of Spain and Portugal.	A. D.
Philip III.	1597
Philip IV.	1621

King of Denmark.	
Christian IV.	1588

Kings of Sweden.	
Sigismund	1592
Charles IX.	1600
Gustavus II.	1611

CHARLES I.

1625—1649. 24 YEARS.

The troubled reign of Charles the First
  Was but a ceaseless strife
'Twixt royalty and parliament,
  Each struggling for its life.

The parliament refused supplies
  For wars that Charles had made,
And he dissolved it, threatening
  To act without its aid.

A tax, "tonnage and poundage" called,
  And "ship-money," he raised,
And then the fire of discontent
  Throughout the country blazed.

Hampden, refusing the demand,
In prison was confined,
But the more fully did his wrongs
Arouse the public mind.

The church of England, verging now
Unto a faith more pure,
By Laud* was loaded with such forms
As it could ill endure.

And on the Scottish church he forced
The English Liturgy;
But everywhere the people rose,
Determined to be free.

A "solemn league and covenant"†
Was signed by high and low;
To arms they rushed, and Charles implored
Aid to repel the blow.

But parliament confined itself
Unto its wrongs alone;
At first it would but limit him,
Now would upset the throne.

Cromwell and Hampden, Pym and Vane,
Were foremost in the strife;

---

* Archbishop of Canterbury.

† Those who signed it were called Covenanters; they were of both sexes, and of all ages.

Laud and Earl Strafford were impeached,
  And both deprived of life.*

In sixteen hundred forty-two
  Commenced a civil war,
And in five years the royalists
  Succumbed on Marston Moor.

A parliament, which Cromwell "purged,"†
  Then sentenced Charles to die,
And through the nation's heart there ran
  A thrill of sympathy.

The Quakers then arose amid
  The turmoil and the strife,
Calling the people from the world
  Unto a holy life.

For the unfaltering maintenance
  Of their religious faith,
They suffered contumely and stripes,
  Imprisonment and death.‡

* The supporters of the king were called Cavaliers; those of the parliament, Roundheads — a name given in derision by their opponents, from the fact that the hair of many of their prominent members was closely cropped, in contradistinction to the fashion of the day. A bowl was put on the head, and the hair cut along the brim of it.

† He expelled the Presbyterians, and called this "*Purging the parliament.*" After this, it was called the "*Rump parliament.*"

‡ It is calculated that forty thousand of this sect died during their

Fox was the founder of the sect,
And preached its simple creed —
A teacher, fearless in the truth,
And pure in thought and deed.

In this reign, Donne* and Drayton* lived;
Quarles,* Fuller,† Barrow,† Taylor,†
Seldon‡ and Coke,§ and Walton, too,
The philosophic angler.

Then was the first post-mail; || it took
Letters one day in seven;
Then the Star-Chamber court¶ dissolved,
Which great offence had given.

---

imprisonment, in consequence of the filth and malaria of the jails, added to cruel treatment. — *Lord's Modern History.*

* Poets. † Theologians.

‡ Antiquarian, historian, jurist. § Distinguished jurist.

|| Established by Charles the First. It ran between London and Edinburgh.

¶ The "Court of the Star-Chamber and High Commission" was instituted for trials by a committee of the privy council, during the reign of Henry VII., in the year 1487. In the reign of Charles I., its arbitrary exactions rendered it odious to the people, and it was abolished by Cromwell's parliament. Coke says, "It probably received its name from its roof being garnished with stars." Goldsmith tells us, "It was so called from the *starra*, or Jewish covenants, deposited there by order of Richard I. No star was admitted as valid, unless found in this depository, and here they remained until the banishment of the Jews by Edward I."

CONTEMPORARY SOVEREIGNS.

Popes.	A. D.	Emperors of the Turks.	A. D.	King of Spain and Portugal.	A. D.
Urban VIII.	1623	Amurath IV.	1623	Philip IV.	1621
Innocent X.	1644	Ibrahim	1649		
		Mahomet IV.	1649		
Emperors of Germany.		**Kings of France.**		**King of Portugal.** (*Alone.*)	
Ferdinand II.	1619	Louis XIII.	1610	John IV.	1640
Ferdinand III.	1637	Louis XIV.	1643		

THE COMMONWEALTH.

1649—1660. 11 YEARS.

The Presbyterians had fought,
Determined to be free,
But now the Independents claimed
The right of sovereignty.

The power which the parliament
Had wrested from the throne,
At length, by Cromwell's management,
The army held alone.

The Scottish Presbyterians
Proclaimed Charles Second then,
And rallied round his standard, with
Full fourteen thousand men.

But Cromwell marched his army there,
Subdued them at *Dunbar*,
At *Worcester* fully conquered them,
And the prince fled afar.

The famous "Navigation Act"
A war with Holland brought;
And England conquered,—Penn and Blake
Against De Ruyter fought.

When the "Long Parliament"* designed
The army to reduce,
Cromwell dissolved it, deeming it
As of no further use.

And then the reins of government
He seized, and held alone;
Wisely he ruled, but regally,
As though upon a throne.

He called a parliament, though not
Elected, as of yore,
And "Praise-God Barebones' Parliament,"†
Was the strange name it bore.

It was dissolved, and Cromwell next
"Protector" claimed to be;
No monarch was in Europe found
More powerful than he.

* It was in session twelve years — hence its name.
† Named from one of its chief actors.

At Tunis, Algiers, everywhere,
  He did the victory gain;
Jamaica island, and the town
  Of Dunkirk, took from Spain.

But foes were upon every side,
  E'en in that triumph hour;
Republican and royalist
  Rebelled against his power.

Richard, his son, succeeded him—
  Was inefficient found;
And next came anarchy, and next
  Was Charles the Second crowned.

In sixteen hundred fifty-five
  Engines by steam were moved;
By Worcester's marquis they were made,
  By Watt they were improved.

CONTEMPORARY SOVEREIGNS.

Popes.	A. D.
Innocent X.	1644
Alexander VII.	1655
Emperors of Germany.	
Ferdinand III.	1637
Leopold	1658
Emperor of the Turks.	
Mahomet IV.	1649

King of France.	A. D.
Louis XIV.	1643
King of Spain.	
Philip IV.	1621
Kings of Portugal.	
John IV.	1640
Alphonso IV.	1656

King of Denmark.	A. D.
Frederick III.	1648
King and Queen of Sweden.	
Christina	1633
Charles X.	1653

RESTORATION OF THE STUARTS.

CHARLES II.

1660—1685. 25 YEARS.

Charles, irreligious, profligate,
And prodigal and vain,
The monarch's character impressed
Itself upon his reign.

Weary of puritanic gloom,
Weary of martial rule,
"High church" or "Tory* principles"
Was the prevailing school.

Episcopacy was restored
Throughout the English land,
And uniformity in faith
A statute did command.

Charles sold Dunkirk,† and squandered all
The money thus obtained;
Warred long and fiercely with the Dutch,
But no advantage gained.

* The epithets, Whig and Tory, originated in this reign; the Tories favoured the claims of the crown, the Whigs, those of the people.

† He received for it four hundred thousand pounds.

Dissolved two parliaments, where Whigs
  Had gained the upper hand:
Plots, intrigues, and conspiracies,
  Were rife throughout the land.

The people, fearing Catholic
  Would be the ruling faith,
For a pretended "Popish Plot,"
  Stafford was put to death.

And of the "Rye-House Plot," a feigned
  Reform conspiracy,
Sidney and Russell were accused,
  And were condemned to die.

In sixty-five, a plague* and fire†
  A frightful havoc made:
Of London city, full three-fourths
  In utter ruin laid.

But Wren,‡ the famous architect,
  Rebuilt the town again;

---

* 68,596 persons died of this pestilence.

† Within the space of four days, eighty-nine churches, (including St. Paul's,) the city gates, the Royal Exchange, the Custom House, Guildhall, Sion College, and many other public buildings, were destroyed, besides 13,200 houses, laying waste 400 streets. — *Hume, Rapin, Carte.*

‡ Sir Christopher Wren.

St. Paul's Cathedral,* too, he built
In this and the next reign.

The famous Habeas Corpus act
Was at this time produced;
Turnpikes were first established then,
And tea was introduced.

Then Waller,† Cowley,† Bunyan‡ lived,
And Baxter § wrote his "Call,"
And Milton his great work composed,
Of the first sin and fall.

CONTEMPORARY SOVEREIGNS.

Popes.	A. D.	Emperor of the Turks.	A. D.	Kings of Portugal.	A. D.
Alexander VII. .	1655	Mahomet IV....	1649	Alphonso IV....	1656
Clement IX.	1667			Pedro II........	1688
Clement X.	1670	**Kings of Spain.**		**Kings of Denmark.**	
Innocent XI.	1676	Philip IV.	1621	Frederick III. ..	1648
		Charles II.	1665	Christian V.....	1670
Emperor of Germany.		**King of France.**		**King of Sweden.**	
Leopold	1658	Louis XIV......	1643	Charles XI.	1660

---

* This cathedral was commenced in 1675, and concluded in thirty-five years; the year that it was finished the architect died, aged ninety-one. James's adherents were called Jacobites.

† Poets.

‡ Author of "Pilgrims' Progress."

§ Theologian.

JAMES II.

1685—1689. 4 YEARS.

The reign of James the Second passed
In weak attempts, and vain,
To crush the English church, and bring
The popish faith again:

And when these inroads on their faith
Had made his object known,
Was Mary importuned to come
And fill her father's throne.

At her approach, James fled to France;
The people flocked around,
And William, prince of Orange, and
Mary, were sovereigns crowned.

The duke of Monmouth, Charles's son,
Aspiring to the throne,
Was killed, with all who aided him,
Wherever they were known.

The Pennsylvania Colony
Was first established then;
It was composed of Quakers, led
By the good William Penn.

The poet Dryden, who ne'er told
  Unwelcome truths in rhyme,
And Boyle, the chemist and the sage,
  Were authors of this time.

CONTEMPORARY SOVEREIGNS.

Pope.	A. D.	King of France.	A. D.	King of Denmark.	A. D.
Innocent XI.	1676	Louis XIV.	1643	Christian V.	1670
Emperor of Germany.		**King of Spain.**		**King of Sweden.**	
Leopold	1658	Charles II.	1665	Charles XI.	1660
Emperors of the Turks.		**King of Portugal.**			
Mahomet IV.	1649	Pedro II.	1668		
Solyman III.	1687				

WILLIAM III. AND MARY.

1689—1702. 13 YEARS.

"The Revolution," this is called,
  "Of sixteen eighty-eight;"
The Protestant succession it
  Secured unto the state;

The rights of parliament secured,
  Religious freedom, too;

The king's prerogative confined
  Within the limits due.

Ireland still adhered to James,
  But France his claim maintained,
Till William, at the river *Boyne*,
  A victory o'er them gained.

And Scotland did her ancient crown
  At William's footstool lay;
The Highlanders alone rebelled,
  Then yielded to his sway.

But from the vale of fair Glencoe
  Rang out a fearful cry,
For slight default, Argyle had doomed
  The whole to butchery.

The "allied army"* fought with France—
  He took the chief command;
At length the "Peace of Ryswick" brought
  Repose unto the land.

Thirty-six million sterling for
  This single war† was paid,
And of the nation's heavy debt
  This the foundation laid.

---

* England, Germany, Holland, and Spain, were leagued together.

† This is called "King William's War," or the "Glorious Revolution of Sixteen Eighty-eight." Its cost to England was £36,000,000.

A Bank* in England first was known
In sixteen ninety-four,
The goldsmiths had retained the gold
Of monied men before.

CONTEMPORARY SOVEREIGNS.

Popes.	A. D.	Emperor of the Turks.	A. D.	Kings of Portugal.	A. D.
Alexander VII.	1655	Mahomet IV.	1649	Alphonso IV.	1656
Clement IX.	1667			Pedro II.	1668
Clement X.	1670	**King of France.**		**Kings of Denmark.**	
Innocent XI.	1676	Louis XIV.	1643	Frederick III.	1648
				Christian V.	1670
Emperor of Germany.		**Kings of Spain.**		**King of Sweden.**	
Leopold	1658	Philip IV.	1621	Charles XI.	1660
		Charles II.	1665		

ANNE I.

1702—1714. 12 YEARS.

Again we note, conspicuous by
The triumphs of the mind,
The *truly great* ones of the earth,—
Newton and Locke we find.

---

* The name is derived from Banco, a bench which was erected in the market-places for the exchange of money. The mint, in the Tower of London, was anciently the depository for the merchants' cash, until Charles the First seized the money, and destroyed the

And in *such* royalty doth lie
  A nation's pride and hope;
In this reign, too, lived Addison,*
  Rowe,† Steel,‡ and Swift§ and Pope.||

De Foe, Guy, Prior, Arbuthnot,
  Charmers of child and sage;
By some historians, this has been
  Called the "Augustan Age."

The women from embroidery turned,
  And learned to study more,
Translating Latin, Spanish, French,
  And Greek and Hebrew lore.¶

---

credit of the mint, 1640. The tradesmen were then driven to some other place of security for their gold, which, when kept at home, their apprentices frequently absconded with to the army. In 1645, they consented to lodge it with the goldsmiths, who were provided with strong iron chests for their own valuable wares, and this was the origin of banking in England. — *Haydn.*

* Essayist — author of the Spectator, the first literary periodical published in England.

† Poet and dramatist.

‡ Essayist and dramatist.

§ Satirist.

|| Poet.

¶ So Harrison, a writer of that day, assures us, giving many names of ladies thus distinguished. The queen was a proficient in all these languages. After describing the various ways in which the ladies employ themselves for recreation from study, "some in exercising their fingers with the needle, divers in spinning of silk, the youngest with their lutes, citterns, pricksong, and all kinds of music, the eldest with skill in surgery and distillation of waters," he adds, "but there are *none of them*, but, when they be at home, can help to supply the

A Constitutional Union now
England and Scotland bound,
And from this time its monarchs were
Kings of Great Britain crowned.

Great Britain joined with Germany
And Holland in a war
Against the king of France, who strove
To spread his conquests far.

Marlborough led the British force,—
The German, Prince Eugene;
At length the peace of "Utrecht" came
In seventeen thirteen.

France was subdued; and England gained
Gibraltar, Hudson's Bay,
Newfoundland, Nova Scotia,—and
She holds them at this day.

Near three and sixty million pounds
This war had cost the land;
Oh, for its suffering poor, how much
Might such a sum command!

The strife of Whig and Tory ran
Higher than e'er was known;
Doctor Sacheverell then preached
Obedience to the throne.

---

ordinary wants of the kitchen with a number of delicate dishes of their own devising."

The Whigs had ruled the parliament,
And filled the ministry;
The Tories, e'er the reign had closed,
Gained the ascendency.

CONTEMPORARY SOVEREIGNS.

Pope.	A. D.	King of France.	A. D.	King of Denmark.	A. D.
Clement XI.....	1700	Louis XIV......	1643	Frederick IV....	1699
Emperors of Germany.		**King of Spain.**		**King of Sweden.**	
Leopold	1658	Philip V........	1700	Charles XII.....	1697
Joseph I........	1705				
Charles VI......	1711				
Emperors of the Turks.		**Kings of Portugal.**		**King of Prussia.**	
Mustapha II....	1695	Pedro II........	1683	Frederick I.....	1701
Achmet III.....	1703	John V.........	1707		

HOUSE OF BRUNSWICK.

GEORGE I.

1714—1727. 13 YEARS.

Without apparent discontent,
King George the First was crowned,
But soon, in James the Second's son,
Was a "Pretender" found.

The English Tories and the Scotch
  Boldly maintained his right;
Some were imprisoned, some were killed,
  But he escaped by flight.

In past reigns war had drained the land,
  And funds had been obtained
From companies of merchants, who
  But small per centage gained.

Blount, of the "South Sea Company,"
  Imposed a golden dream,
Then bought the debts, and thousands fell
  By this the "South Sea Scheme."

The streets of London being still
  Without sufficient lights,
Each house was ordered to hang out
  A lamp on moonless nights.

CONTEMPORARY SOVEREIGNS.

Popes.	A. D.	Emperor of the Turks.	A. D.	Empress of Russia.	A. D.
Clement XI.	1700	Achmet III.	1703	Catherine I.	1725
Innocent XIII.	1721			**Kings of France.**	
Benedict XIII.	1724	**Emperor of Russia.**		Louis XIV.	1643
Emperor of Germany.		Peter the Great, first emperor	1702	Louis XV.	1715
Charles VI.	1711			**King of Spain.**	
				Philip V.	1700

GEORGE II.

1727—1760. 33 YEARS.

For ten years after George was crowned
  Did peace triumphant reign,
When, with scarce shadow for excuse,
  A war was broached with Spain.

Then, to support the Austrian queen,
  Another war* was waged,
And in this contest greater part
  Of Europe was engaged.

The treaty of Aix-la-Chapelle
  Settled Theresa's claim;
But while King George made war abroad,
  The young "Pretender" came:

And, aided by the king of France,
  Twice did he gain the field,
But at *Culloden*, in the fight,
  He was compelled to yield.

He fled, and wandered through the land,
  Unsheltered and alone;
The Stuarts made no more attempts
  To gain the English throne.

* This war was called the "War of the Austrian Succession;" it cost England £54,000,000.

In North America did France
On Britain's soil intrude,
And, seventeen hundred fifty-five,
A war* with her ensued.

At first the French were conquerors,
But at its close did they
Surrender all of Canada
Unto the British sway.

In India the British had
Extended wide their trade,
And their "East India Company"
Frequent encroachments made.

The natives rose resistingly,
But vain their efforts all;
They lost Bahar, Orissa, and
The kingdom of Bengal.

In seventeen hundred fifty-two
New style was introduced;
In England first in twenty-one
Inoculation used.†

---

* This war closed with the "Peace of Paris," Feb. 10th, 1763, the third year of the reign of George III.

† Introduced from Turkey in 1721 by Lady Mary Wortley Montague. She had her own son inoculated, and was afterwards allowed to have it tried upon seven condemned criminals.

In twenty-nine, the Methodists*
  First into notice came,—
Wesley and Whitfield preached their faith,
  Warmed by a holy flame.

Watts,† Thompson,† Young,† Goldsmith,† and
    Gray,‡
  In this reign lived and wrote;
Hume,§ Collins,|| Akenside,|| and Sterne,
  With many more of note.

First Horace Walpole exercised
  The ministerial sway,
And Pitt, the earl of Chatham, last
  Great statesman of his day.

Then Rysback,¶ Reynolds,** Wilson,†† lived,
  Doddridge‡‡ and Dodsley,‡‡ too,
Halley,§§ Hogarth,|||| Howard,¶¶ and
  The Lady Montague.***

---

* The name was suggested by the Latin appellation Methodistæ, given to a college of physicians in ancient Rome, in consequence of the strict regimen under which they placed their patients.

† Poets and miscellaneous writers.

‡ Poet. § Historian. || Popular poets.

¶ (John Michael) sculptor.

** (Sir Joshua) painter. Died 1792.

†† (Richard) landscape painter. Died 1782.

‡‡ Poets. §§ Astronomer.

|||| (William) painter. Died 1764.

¶¶ (John) celebrated philanthropist. Died 1790.

*** (Mary Wortley) distinguished writer.

CONTEMPORARY SOVEREIGNS.

Popes.

	A. D.
Benedict XIII. . .	1724
Clement XII. . . .	1738
Benedict XIV. . .	1740
Clement XIII. . .	1758

Emperors of Germany.

Charles VI.	1711
Charles VII.	1740
Francis Stephen	1745

Emperors and Empresses of Russia.

	A. D.
Peter II.	1727
Anne	1730
John	1740
Elizabeth	1741

King of France.

Louis XV.	1715

Kings of Spain.

Philip V. (res.) . .	1724
Ferdinand VI. . .	1745

Emperors of the Turks.

Achmet III.	1703
Mahomet V.	1730
Osman II.	1754
Mustapha III. . .	1757

Kings of Portugal.

	A. D.
John V.	1707
Joseph	1750

Kings of Denmark.

Frederick IV. . . .	1699
Christian VI. . . .	1730
Frederick V. . . .	1746

Kings of Sweden.

Frederick	1720
Adolphus	1750

Kings of Prussia.

Frederick II. . . .	1713
Frederick III. . . .	1740

GEORGE III.

1760—1820. 60 YEARS.

The ministry of George the Third
A policy pursued,
Unto America unjust,
And thence a war ensued.

Her Independence she declared,
Resolved to do and dare,—
The shackles of a foreign king
No longer would she wear.

No longer be controlled by laws
She had not helped to frame;
No longer taxed by parliament,
Where she had not a name.

In seventy-five, a war commenced,
And, seventeen eighty-three,
She was victorious, and the king
Yielded his sovereignty.

Her victory thrilled the heart of France,
And its crushed masses rose
In war upon the church and state,
Their unrelenting foes.

From slumber long and deep, the kings
Of Europe roused to know
That from the people, scorned so long,
Might spring the deadliest foe.

They hastened to the field, and stood
An army close "allied,"
And goaded France to desperate deeds,
Till blood flowed far and wide.

Then, like a tempest, Bonaparte
Rushing through Europe came,
Ambitious, as a conqueror,
To build himself a name:

He crushed the crowns beneath his feet,
  And rocked the empires round,
Till listening Europe recognised
  But war's terrific sound.

England against *Republic* France
  Had constant battle made,
And now against *Imperial* France
  Her forces were arrayed.

She joined the nations, or she fought
  The desperate fight alone,
Resolved nor blood nor gold to spare,
  'Till victory was won.

Her Nelson conquered on the seas,
  With France and Spain at war —
First, in the "Battle of the Nile,"
  And last at *Trafalgar*.

Talavera, *Salamanca*,
  Vittoria, *Waterloo*,
Were battles where Lord Wellington
  Made her triumphant, too.

On Waterloo the contest closed,
  Which had for twenty years
Made Europe one great battle-field,
  And drenched her soil with tears.

For war, since sixteen eighty-eight,*
Has England paid, 'tis found,
Two billion, twenty million, and
Five hundred thousand pound.

In India, Great Britain fought,
Extending wide her sway,
O'er Hyder Ally conquering,
But carnage marked her way.

Against her power had Ireland,
In ninety-two, rebelled;
France aided, but Cornwallis soon
The insurrection quelled.

A union at length was formed
In eighteen hundred one,
And England, Scotland, Ireland, were
Then as "Great Britain" known.

America, in eighteen twelve,
War upon England made;
England her seamen had impressed,
And had disturbed her trade.

---

* The period of the revolution which seated William and Mary upon the throne.

For this, the horrors of three years
  Of warfare she endured;
She partly conquered on the seas,
  And then was peace procured.

The Algerines, as pirates, were
  Notorious near and far,
And their inhuman law made slaves
  Of prisoners of war.

An English fleet assailed their coast,
  And only granted peace
Upon the terms that slavery should
  In their dominion cease.

And she abolished, in the year
  Of eighteen hundred seven,
Her foreign slave-trade,* — piracy,
  None baser under Heaven!

Though poets wrote to gain this end,
  And politicians, too,
To Clarkson, Sharpe, and Wilberforce,
  Is the great merit due.

---

* It was shown by authentic documents, produced by government, that from 1792 to 1807, a period of fifteen years, upwards of three millions, five hundred thousand Africans had been taken from their country, and had either miserably perished on the passage, or been sold in the West Indies. — *Butler.*

This reign was marked by vigorous thought—
By rapid progress made
In navigation, letters, arts,
In wealth, in power and trade.

There we find Gibbon,* Robertson,*
Fox,† Sheridan,† and Tooke,‡
Johnson,§ Burke,† Blackstone,|| Adam Smith,¶
Cowper,** Bruce,†† Burns,** and Cook.‡‡

Priestley,§§ Horne,|||| Paley,¶¶ Reynolds,***
Reid,†††
Stewart,‡‡‡ Brown,§§§ More,|||||| and
Blair,¶¶¶
Herschell,**** Bell,†††† Davy,‡‡‡‡ Byron,**
White,**
Shelley,** and Keats,** were there.

---

* Historian.
† Statesman and orator.
‡ (Horne) philosopher.
§ Lexicographer.
|| Eminent lawyer.
¶ Political economist.
** Poet.
†† Traveller.
‡‡ Navigator.
§§ Philosopher and writer.
|||| Theologian.
¶¶ Metaphysician.
*** Painter.
††† Metaphysician, poet, essayist, and moralist.
‡‡‡ Philosopher.
§§§ Philosophical writer.
|||||| (Hannah) essayist and moralist.
¶¶¶ Theologian and rhetorician.
**** Astronomer.
†††† Surgeon, anatomist, and physiologist.
‡‡‡‡ Chemist.

The Spinning Jenny* first was used
In seventeen sixty-nine;
In eighty-five, the stages first
Carried the written line.

In seventeen hundred ninety-eight
Was vaccination used;†
In eighteen hundred and fourteen
Was gas first introduced.

A locomotive-engine first
In eighteen four was seen;
The first steamboat, in England, built
In eighteen and fifteen.

In sixteen, Davy's Safety Lamp
The venturous miner saved;
In eighteen, pictures upon steel
By Perkins were engraved.

---

* The first spinning jenny was made by Hargreaves, of Lancashire, 1767; it was improved by Sir Richard Arkwright, and a patent taken out, in 1769. Cotton was formerly spun by the hand.

† Discovered by Dr. Jenner.

CONTEMPORARY SOVEREIGNS.

Popes.	A. D.
Clement XIV. . .	1769
Pius VI.	1775
Pius VII.	1800

Emperors of Germany.	
Joseph II.	1765
Leopold II.	1790
Francis II.	1792
Assumed the title of Emperor of Austria.	

Emperors of the Turks.	A. D.
Mustapha III. . . .	1757
Achmet IV.	1774
Selim III.	1789
Mahmoud VI. . .	1808

Emperors and Empresses of Russia.	
Peter III.	1762
Catherine II. . . .	1763
Paul I.	1797
Alexander	1801

Sovereigns of France.	A. D.
Louis XVI.	1774
Republic	1793
Napoleon, Consul	1799
" Emperor	1804
Louis XVIII. . . .	1814

Kings of Spain.	
Charles III.	1759
Charles IV.	1788
Ferdinand VII. .	1808

GEORGE IV.

1820—1830. 10 YEARS.

George Fourth arraigned his queen for crimes,
But proof he could not find,
And to deprive her of her rights,
The House of Lords declined.

Hostilities had ceased, but wars'
Encumbrances remained,
And various speculative schemes
Unwonted credence gained.

In twenty-five, the "bubbles"* burst,
And vanished into air,—
Four hundred thousand sterling pounds
Were represented there.

England refused her aid to France
To tyrannize in Spain,
But she assisted Greece, who strove
Her freedom to regain.

With Russia and with France allied,
She fought the Turkish fleet,—
In *Navarino* harbour gained
A victory complete.

For years had Greece been suffering
Beneath the Turkish yoke,
But now she rose exultingly—
Her galling fetters broke.

In Africa and India
Were insurrections quelled,
For still against their conquerors
The colonists rebelled.

A Bill, providing that the laws
No longer should remain
To Roman Catholics opposed,
Distinguished this reign.

---

* This has been styled "the year of the disastrous speculation in *bubbles*."

Macadamizing London streets
In twenty-four began,
And carriages, propelled by steam,
In twenty-nine first ran.

Then Coleridge,* Crabbe,* and Southey,† lived,
Hemans,‡ Hogg,§ Hall,|| and Scott,¶
Lander** and Lamb,†† with more whose names
Will long be unforgot.

CONTEMPORARY SOVEREIGNS.

POPE. A. D.
Leo XII 1823

EMPEROR OF AUSTRIA.
Francis........ 1804

KING OF BAVARIA.
Louis Charles Augustus 1825

KING OF THE NETHERLANDS.
William I...... 1813

KING AND ELECTORATE OF BOHEMIA.
Francis II...... 1792

KING OF DENMARK.
Frederick VI. .. 1808

KING OF FRANCE.
Charles X...... 1824

KING OF PRUSSIA. A. D.
Frederick III. .. 1797

KING OF HANOVER.
George IV. king of Great Britain . 1820

KINGS OF NAPLES AND SICILY.
Ferdinand IV. (restored).... 1824
Francis Janvier Joseph 1825

KING OF SPAIN.
Ferdinand VII. . 1808

KING OF POLAND.
Nicholas I., see Russia 1825

QUEEN OF PORTUGAL. A. D.
Donna Maria da Gloria....... 1831

EMPEROR OF RUSSIA.
Nicholas I...... 1825

KING OF SARDINIA.
Charles Felix... 1821

KING OF SAXONY.
Anthony Clement 1827

KING OF SWEDEN AND NORWAY.
Charles XIV.... 1818

GRAND SEIGNIOR OF TURKEY.
Mahmoud VI. .. 1808

KING OF WIRTEMBERG.
Frederick William 1816

---

* Poets. † Poet, historian, and biographer. ‡ Poetess.
§ (Ettrick Shepherd) poet. || Eminent divine.
¶ Novelist, poet, historian, and biographer.
** African traveller. †† Essayist.

WILLIAM IV.

1830—1837. 7 YEARS.

When William, brother to the king,
  Succeeded to the throne,
The people had resolved to make
  Their heavy grievance known.

War had increased the nation's debt
  Beyond its power to pay,
And 'neath the taxes, quadrupled,
  The groaning people lay.

They urged upon the parliament
  That members should be sent
More from the counties and the towns,
  Their rights to represent.

The duke of Wellington resigned,
  Grey fought the battle through,
And the "Reform Bill" passed at length
  In eighteen thirty-two.

Reform was gained for Ireland, too,
  Where great distress prevailed;
She sought to be relieved from tithes,—
  But here her efforts failed.

To use the surplus of this fund
  To aid the public good
The Commons moved, but in the House
  Of Lords it was withstood.

O'Connell preached throughout the land
  The Union repeal,
And urged it as the only means
  The nation's wounds to heal.

But the great fact in William's reign
  On which the Christian smiles,
Is that eight hundred thousand slaves,
  In the West India isles,

Were loosed in eighteen thirty-four
  By parliament's decree,
And twenty millions sterling paid
  To set the bondman free.

In England's annals, this is found
  To be the only reign
In which no foreign war was waged,
  No man for treason slain.

ALEXANDRINA VICTORIA.

BEGAN TO REIGN JUNE 20TH, 1837.

Shouts rent the air, and far and near
  Were joyful faces seen,
When to the English throne advanced
  A fair and youthful queen.

Ere long, disturbances arose
  In Canada, and war
Has since been waged with Syria,
  With China and Lahore.

In the wide question of "Repeal,"
  All Ireland has engaged;
Frightfully famine and disease,
  And civil war, have raged.

The reformation long required
  In Corn laws has been made,
And England has adopted now
  The system of Free trade.*

* It is thought correct to say she has adopted the *system* of free trade. She has no "*protective* tax"—no tax to protect her own manufactures; but an "*income* tax" and a tax on goods imported, (such as she does not grow,) to produce a revenue. This tax averages 10 per cent., excepting on tobacco, which pays 300 per cent.

The working classes have combined,
 Their wrongs have been revealed,
Five millions of the "Chartists"* have
 To parliament appealed.

The tax on window-panes has been
 Abolished in this reign;
The "Penny Postage system" doth
 Throughout the realm obtain.†

Vessels propelled by steam have first
 An ocean passage made,
And the Electric Telegraph‡
 The message has conveyed.

England has mourned the great and good,
 Passed from the earth away,—

* So called from the Charter which they presented to parliament. Their chief demands are, Universal suffrage, Vote by ballot, No property qualification for voting, Annual parliaments, Payment of members, and Equal Electoral districts.

† Established in 1840.

‡ England and France are now connected by electric telegraph wires cased in gutta percha, which were sunk in the channel, from Dover to Cape Geisnez, Aug. 28th, 1850. The sea here is from 30 to 180 feet deep. The number of miles of telegraphic lines in Great Britain in 1849, all on railway tracks, was 2000. The cost, $750 per mile.

Philanthropists, philosophers,
  Poets, and statesmen, they.*

But those yet live, whose minds and hearts
  Would honour any age,—
Whose names, in days that are to come,
  Will brighten history's page.

Efforts are making to diffuse
  Learning amongst the poor,
And to repeal the olden "Law
  Of Primogeniture."†

---

* Among the distinguished individuals who have died since the commencement of this reign, are:—

Letitia McClean (L. E. Landon), Poet............ 1838
Costley Paxton Cooper, M. D., Medical Writer........ 1840
Robert Southey, Poet, Historian, and Biographer.... 1843
Thomas Campbell, Poet... 1844
Thomas Henderson, Astronomer............... 1844
Thomas Hood, Poet....... 1845
Elizabeth Fry, Philanthropist.................. 1845
R. B. Haydon, Painter..... 1846
Thomas Chalmers, D. D., Theologian and Political Economist............ 1846
Daniel O'Connell......... 1847
D'Israeli, Literateur....... 1848
Thomas Dick, Astronomer. 1849
Maria Edgeworth, Novelist 1849
Cooke Taylor, Historian... 1849
Horace Smith, Literateur.. 1849
Lord Eldon.............. 1849
W. L. Bowles, Poet....... 1849
Sir William Allen, Painter. 1849
W. Prout, Chemist........ 1849
Jane Porter, Novelist...... 1849
W. Kirby, Entomologist.... 1849
William Wordsworth, Poet 1850
R. Westall, Painter....... 1850
R. J. Wyatt, Sculptor...... 1850
Sir M. A. Shee, Painter.... 1850
P. F. Tyler, Historian..... 1850
Joanna Baillie, Poet and Novelist................. 1851
Ebenezer Elliot, Author of "Corn Law Rhymes"... 1851
Sir Robert Peel, Prime Minister of England, July, 1851
Thomas Moore, Poet...... 1852

† This law was introduced by William the Conqueror.

The right of Franchise to extend,—
  The Jews to free from all
The legal disabilities
  Which hold them now in thrall.

And for the delver in the mine,
  The toiler at the loom,
The convict in the prison-cell,
  Light breaketh through the gloom.

Great Britain challenges the world,
  And worketh what she will;
In commerce, all unrivalled she,
  And in industrial skill.

In science, literature, and arts,
  She has a glorious fame;
Unto the sea's wide sovereignty,
  Europe accords her claim.

For bridges, roads, canals, no land
  Can with her own compare;
In unsurpassed magnificence
  Arise her buildings fair.

On every sea her sail is spread,
  In every port 'tis furled,—
The "*Land of Tin*" has now become
  The wonder of the world!

CHRONOLOGICAL CHART,

TABLES, &c.

REIGNING SOVEREIGNS OF EUROPE.

Name.	Title.	State.	Date of Birth.	Date of Accession.	Age at Accession.	Religion.
Oscar I.	King	Sweden and Norway.	July 4, 1799	Mar. 8, 1844	45	Lutheran.
Nicholas I.	Emperor	Russia	July 6, 1796	Dec. 1, 1825	29	Gr'k Church.
Frederick VII.	King	Denmark	Oct. 6, 1808	Jan. 20, 1848	39	Lutheran.
Victoria	Queen	Great Britain	May 24, 1819	June 20, 1837	18	Prot. Episc.
William III.	King	Holland or Netherl'ds	Feb. 19, 1817	Mar. 17, 1849	32	Reformed.
Leopold	"	Belgium	Dec. 16, 1790	July 21, 1831	40	Lutheran.*
Frederick Wm. IV.	"	Prussia	Oct. 15, 1795	June 7, 1840	45	Evangelical.
Frederick Augustus	"	Saxony	May 18, 1797	June 6, 1836	39	Catholic.*
Ernest Augustus	"	Hanover	May 27, 1819	1851	33	Evangelical.
Frederick Francis	Grand Duke	Mecklenburg-Schwer.	Feb. 28, 1823	Mar. 7, 1842	19	Lutheran.
George	" "	Mecklenburg-Strelitz	Aug. 12, 1799	Nov. 6, 1816	37	"
Augustus	" "	Oldenburg	July, 13, 1783	May 21, 1829	46	"
William	Duke	Brunswick	Apr. 25, 1806	Apr. 25, 1831	25	"
Adolphus	"	Nassau	July 24, 1817	Aug. 20, 1839	22	Evangelical.
Charles Frederick	Grand Duke	Saxe-Weimar-Eisen	Feb. 2, 1783	June 14, 1828	45	Lutheran.
Ernest II	Duke	Saxe-Coburg-Gotha	June 21, 1818	Jan. 29, 1844	26	"
Bernard	"	Saxe-Meiningen	Dec. 17, 1800	Dec. 24, 1803	3	"

REIGNING SOVEREIGNS OF EUROPE.—Continued.

Name.	Title.	State.	Date of Birth.	Date of Accession.	Age at Accession.	Religion.
Joseph	Duke	Saxe-Altenburg	Aug. 27, 1789	Sept. 29, 1834	45	Lutheran.
Leopold	"	Anhalt-Dessau	Oct. 1, 1794	Aug. 9, 1817	22	Evangelical.
Alexander	"	Anhalt-Bernberg	Mar. 2, 1805	Mar. 24, 1834	29	"
Augusta	Duchess	Anhalt-Cöthen	Aug. 3, 1794	Nov. 23, 1847	53	Reformed.
Gunther	Prince	Schwarzburg-Rudolst.	Nov. 6, 1793	Apr. 28, 1807	13	Lutheran.
Gunther	"	Schwarzburg-Sonder'n	Sept. 24, 1801	Sept. 3, 1835	34	"
Henry XX.........	"	Reuss, (Elder Line)..	June 29, 1794	Oct. 31, 1836	42	"
Henry LXII.	"	Reuss, (Younger Line)	May 31, 1785	Apr. 17, 1818	33	"
Leopold	"	Lippe-Detmold	Nov. 6, 1796	Apr. 4, 1802	5	Reformed.
George	"	Lippe-Schaumburg ...	Dec. 20, 1784	Feb. 13, 1787	2	"
George Victor	"	Waldeck	Jan. 14, 1831	May 15, 1845	14	Evangelical.
Ferdinand	Landgrave ..	Hesse-Homburg	Apr. 26, 1783	Sept. 7, 1848	65	Reformed.
Leopold	Grand Duke	Baden	Aug. 29, 1790	Mar. 30, 1830	40	Evangelical.
Frederick William.	Elector	Hesse-Cassel	Aug. 20, 1802	Nov. 20, 1847	45	Reformed.
Louis III.	Grand Duke	Hesse-Darmstadt	June 9, 1806	June 16, 1848	42	Lutheran.
Charles Antony	Prince	Hohenzol'n-Sigmar'n .	Sept. 7, 1811	Aug. 1848	37	Catholic.
Frederick	"	Hohenzol'n-Hechn'n ..	Feb. 16, 1801	Sept. 13, 1838	37	"
Aloys	"	Lichtenstein	May 26, 1796	Apr. 20, 1836	40	"
William	King	Wurtemberg	Sept. 27, 1781	Oct. 30, 1816	35	Lutheran.
Maximilian II.	"	Bavaria	Nov. 28, 1811	Mar. 21, 1848	37	Catholic.
Francis Joseph I. ..	Emperor ...	Austria	Aug. 18, 1830	Dec. 2, 1848	18	"

REIGNING SOVEREIGNS OF EUROPE.—Continued.

Name.	Title.	State.	Date of Birth.	Date of Accession.	Age at Accession.	Religion.
Charles Louis N. Bonaparte	President...	France	Apr. 20, 1808	Dec. 20, 1848	40	Catholic.
Isabella II.	Queen	Spain	Oct. 10, 1830	Sept. 29, 1833	3	"
Maria II	"	Portugal	Apr. 4, 1819	May 2, 1826	7	"
Victor Emanuel	King	Sardinia	Mar. 14, 1820	Mar. 25, 1849	29	"
Leopold II.	Grand Duke	Tuscany	Oct. 3, 1797	June 18, 1824	26	"
Ferdinand Charles	Duke	Parma	Jan. 14, 1823	April, 1849	26	"
Francis V.	"	Modena and Massa	June 1, 1819	Jan. 21, 1846	26	"
Pius IX.	Pope	States of the Church	May 13, 1792	June 21, 1846	54	"
Ferdinand II.	King	Two Sicilies	Jan. 12, 1810	Nov. 8, 1830	20	"
Otho	"	Greece	June 1, 1815	May 7, 1832	17	Catholic,*
Abdul Medjed	Sultan	Turkey	May 6, 1822	July 1, 1839	17	Mahometan.
Florestan	Prince	Monaco	Oct. 10, 1785	Oct. 2, 1841	56	Catholic.
John	Regent	German Federation	Jan. 20, 1782	June 29, 1848	66	

* The king of Belgium is a *Protestant*, though his subjects are mostly *Catholics;* the king of Saxony is a *Catholic*, though the greater part of his subjects are *Protestants;* and the king of Greece is a *Catholic*, though most of his subjects are of the *Greek Church.*

SOVEREIGNS OF ENGLAND.

SAXON FAMILY.—17 KINGS.

	Kings.	Began to Reign.	Queens.	Issue.
800	EGBERT	827	*Redburga*	*Ethelbert*, ETHELWOLF.*
9th Century.	ETHELWOLF	838	1. ———	ETHELBALD, ETHELBERT.
			2. Judith of France	ETHELRED I., ALFRED.
	ETHELBALD	857	Judith, mother-in-law	*No issue.*
	ETHELBERT	860	*Not known*	*Adhelm*, *Athelward.*
	ETHELRED I.	866		
	ALFRED *the Great.*	872	Aswinta	EDWARD, *Elfleda*, *Ethelwald.**
900	EDWARD *the Elder*	900	1. Elfleda. 2. Edgiva	ATHELSTAN, *Beatrix*, EDMUND I., Edred, *Egitha.**
10th Century.	ATHELSTAN	925		*No issue.*
	EDMUND I.	941	Elgiva	EDWY, EDGAR.
	EDRED	948	*Not known*	Alfrid, Bedfrid.
	EDWY	955	Elgiva	*No issue.*
	EDGAR	959	1. Ethelfleda. 2. Elfrida	EDWARD, ETHELRED II.*
	EDWARD *the Martyr*	975	*Not married.*	
	ETHELRED II.	978	1. Elgiva. 2. Emma of Normandy	EDMUND II., EDWARD.
1000	SWEYN (*Dane*)	1013	1. *Gunilda.* 2. *Sigrita*	CANUTE, *Esthritha.*
	EDMUND II., *Ironside*	1016	*Algitha*	Edmund, Edward the Outlaw, Margaret.

* The asterisk signifies that there was more issue, but not important in history.

DANISH KINGS.—3.

	Kings.	Began Reign.	Queens.	Issue.
11th Century.	CANUTE, *the Great*	1017	1. *Alfwen.* 2. Emma ...	*Sweyn*, HAROLD I., CANUTE II.
	HAROLD I.	1036	*Not married.*	
	CANUTE II.	1039	*Not married.*	

SAXON LINE RESTORED.

	Kings.	Began Reign.	Queens.	Issue.
	EDWARD, *the Confessor*	1041	*Editha*, daughter of Earl Godwin	*No issue.*
	HAROLD II.	1066	1. ———. 2. *Algetha* .	*Edmund, Godwin.*

NORMAN FAMILY.—3 KINGS.

William I., the 7th duke of Normandy, illegitimate son of Robert, and descended from Rollo, the first duke.

	Kings.	Began Reign.	Queens.	Issue.
	WILLIAM I., *the Conqueror*	1066	Matilda of Flanders ...	Robert, Wm II., Henry I., *Adela*, married *Earl of Blois; issue* Stephen, *Family of Blois.*
	WILLIAM II., *Rufus*	1087	*Not married.*	
1100	HENRY I., *Beauclerc*	1100	Matilda of Scotland ...	William, *Matilda*, or *Maud*,* mother of HENRY II.

HOUSE OF BLOIS.—1 KING.

	Kings.	Began Reign.	Queens.	Issue.
	STEPHEN (*grandson*)	1135	Matilda of Boulogne ...	Eustace, William.*

FAMILY OF PLANTAGENET OR ANJOU.—14 KINGS.

Matilda, or Maud, daughter of Henry I., first married Henry V., Emperor of Germany; afterwards, Geoffrey Plantagenet, Earl of Anjou; issue, Henry II.

Century	Kings.	Began Reign.	Queens.	Issue.
12th Century.	HENRY II. (*grandson.*)	1154	Eleanor of Guienne	Henry, RICHARD I., Geoffrey, JOHN, *Matilda.** (From *Matilda*, the present House of *Brunswick* is descended.)
	RICHARD I., *Cœur-de-Lion*	1189	Berenguela of Navarre	*No issue.*
1200 13th Century.	John, *Lackland*	1199	1. Alice. 2. Avisa 3. Isabel	HENRY III., Jane, Isabel, Eleanor, RICHARD.*
	HENRY III.	1216	Eleanor of Provence	EDWARD I., Margaret, Beatrix, Edmund.*
	EDWARD I., *Longshanks*	1272	1. Eleanor of Castile 2. Mary of France	EDWARD II., Thomas, Edmund, Margaret.*
1300	EDWARD II.	1307	Isabella of France	EDWARD III., Jane, Eleanor.
14th Century.	EDWARD III.	1327	Philippa of Hainault	*Edward*, the Black Prince, father of RICHARD II., William, Lionel, (*York*); John of Gaunt, father of HENRY IV., Edmund.
	RICHARD II. (*grandson.*)	1377	1. Anne of Bohemia 2. Isabella of France	*No issue.*

BRANCH OF LANCASTER.—3 KINGS.

John of Gaunt, Duke of Lancaster, fourth son of Edward III.; issue, Henry IV.

	Kings.	Began Reign.	Queens.	Issue.
1400	Henry IV. (*grandson.*)	1399	1. Mary Bohun 2. Jane of Navarre	Henry V., Thomas, John, Humphrey.*
	Henry V.	1413	Catherine of France	Henry VI.
	Henry VI.	1422	Margaret of Anjou	Edward, *murdered.*

BRANCH OF YORK.—3 KINGS.

Lionel, Duke of Clarence, third son of Edward III.; issue, Philippa (married Mortimer, Earl of Marche); issue, Roger; issue, Anne (married Richard, Duke of York, son of Edmund, the fifth son of Edward III.); issue, Richard; issue, Edward IV. and Richard III.

	Kings.	Began Reign.	Queens.	Issue.
15th Century.	Edward IV. (*6th gen.*)	1461	Elizabeth Woodville, or Grey	Edward V., Richard, *Elizabeth*, Catherine.*
	Edward V.	1483	*Not married.*	
	Richard III. (*6th gen.*)	1483	Ann Neville	Edward.

HOUSE OF TUDOR.—5 SOVEREIGNS.

John of Gaunt; issue (second son), John; issue, John; issue, Margaret (married Edmund Tudor); issue, Henry VII.

Century	Kings.	Began Reign.	Queens.	Issue.
	HENRY VII. (5th. gen.)	1485	Elizabeth of York	Arthur (died 1502), HENRY VIII., *Margaret*, Mary,* *grandmother of Jane Grey.*
1500	HENRY VIII.	1509	1. Catharine of Arragon	MARY.
			2. Anne Boleyn	ELIZABETH.
			3. Jane Seymour	EDWARD VI.
			4. Ann of Cleves.	
			5. Catharine Howard.	
			6. Catharine Parr.	
16th Century.	EDWARD VI.	1547	*Not married.*	
	MARY	1553	Philip II., of Spain	*No issue.*
	ELIZABETH	1558	*Not married.*	

FAMILY OF STUART.—6 SOVEREIGNS.

Margaret, daughter of Henry VII., married James IV. (Stuart) of Scotland; issue, James V.; issue, Mary; issue, James VI. of Scotland, same as James I., England.

Century	Kings.	Began Reign.	Queens.	Issue.
1600	JAMES I. (gr. gr. grandson.)	1603	Anne of Denmark	Henry (died 1612), CHARLES I., *Elizabeth.*
	CHARLES I.	1625	Henrietta of France	CHARLES II., JAMES II., Henry, Mary,* *married the Prince of Orange.*

Century	Sovereign	Accession	Married	Issue
17th Century.	*Oliver Cromwell*	1653		(*Protector of the Commonwealth.*)
	CHARLES II.	1660	Catharine of Portugal	*No lawful issue.*
	JAMES II.	1685	1. Ann Hyde. 2. Mary of Este	MARY, ANNE, *James*,* (*Pretender*, father of *Charles Edward, second Pretender*.)
	WILLIAM III. and MARY	1689	MARY, (*daughter of James II., died* 1694)	(WILLIAM III., Prince of Orange, was grandson of Charles I., and husband of MARY.)
1700	ANNE	1702	George, Pr. of Denmark	17 children—all died young.

HOUSE OF BRUNSWICK, HANOVER, OR GUELPH.—6 SOVEREIGNS.

Elizabeth, daughter of James I., married Frederick V., Elector Palatine; issue, Sophia (married Ernest Augustus, Elector of Hanover); issue, George I.

Century	Sovereign	Accession	Married	Issue
18th Century.	GEORGE I. (*gr. grandson.*)	1714	Sophia of Zelle	GEORGE II., Sophia.
	GEORGE II.	1727	Caroline of Anspach	*Frederick*, (father of George III., died 1751,) William, Anne, Louisa.*
	GEORGE III. (*grandson.*)	1760	Charlotte of Mecklenburg-Strelitz	GEORGE IV., Frederick, WILLIAM, Edward, *Ernest Augustus, Adolphus*.*
1800	GEORGE IV.	1820	Caroline of Brunswick	Charlotte Augusta, *died* 1817.
	WILLIAM IV.	1830	Adelaide of Saxe-Meiningen	
19th Century.	ALEXANDRINA VICTORIA	JUNE 10 1837	Married, Feb. 10, 1840, to Prince Albert Augustus Charles Emanuel, of Saxe-Coburg and Gotha, born Aug. 26, 1819.	Victoria, Albert, Alice, Alfred, Helena, Louisa, Arthur.

STATISTICS,

DESCRIPTIVE OF THE PRESENT CONDITION OF GREAT BRITAIN.

Total area of the United Kingdom of Great Britain and Ireland.

	Sq. Miles.	Pop. in 1851.
England	58,648	16,965,684
Scotland	31,268	2,870,784
Wales	7,263	1,100,000
Ireland	28,095	6,515,794
Great Britain and Ireland	125,274	27,452,262

London	about	2,000,000
Liverpool	"	300,000
Edinburgh and Leith	"	200,000
Glasgow	"	300,000
Manchester	"	320,000

The possessions of Great Britain in Europe are:
Heligoland, Gibraltar, and the Ionian Isles.

In Africa.

Senegambia and Upper Guinea, Cape Colony, St. Helena, Mauritius, &c.

In Asia.

Hindostan, part of Farther India, Ceylon, Singapore, Hongkong, &c.

In Australasia.

Australia, Van Diemen's Land, New Zealand, and Norfolk Island.

In America.

British North America, Guiana, many of the West India Islands, Bahamas, and Balize.

Total area of these possessions, 4,686,000 miles. Total population in 1844, 131,000,000.

National Debt	£800,000,000
Revenue for the year ending Jan. 5, 1850	52,951,748
Expenditure	50,853,622

Exports of Great Britain and Ireland, 1849, £58,848,042, being an increase of £9,902,717 over those of 1848.

Of the exports, there were:

To British Colonies	£16,594,037
United States of America	9,564,909
Brazil	2,067,299
China	1,445,959
Cuba	733,169
Mexico and Central South America	3,757,463

Annual Produce.	Value.
Cotton	£35,000,000
Woollen	22,000,000
Iron and Wood ware	17,000,000
Watches, Jewelry, &c.	3,000,000
Leather	13,500,000
Linen	8,000,000
Silk	10,000,000
Glass and Earthen ware	4,250,000
Paper	1,500,000
Hats	2,400,000
Total	£116,650,000

(*McCulloch.*)

Value of the Agricultural Produce, exclusive of Wood.

England and Wales	£132,500,000
Scotland	20,455,000
Ireland	44,500,000
Total	£197,455,000

These estimates must be regarded as mere approximations, though we are disposed to think they come pretty near the mark.—*McCulloch.*

There must, necessarily, be a great deal of looseness in such computations, though we do not believe that the result involves any very material error. There are no means of forming any tolerable correct estimate of the extent of land under different crops in Ireland. — *Ib.*

It is supposed that, of the 8,500,000 people in Ireland, 50,000 are mainly supported by the potatoe; and that, of the remainder, 2,500,000 depend principally upon oats. — *Ib.*

Spirits, 1840.

In England, Ireland, and Scotland, duty was paid in 1840 on the following quantities of spirits, viz:—

	GALLONS.
Rum	2,830,263
Brandy	1,167,756
Geneva	18,640
On other foreign spirits	8,758
On British, Irish, and Scotch spirits	25,190,843

Making, in the whole, nearly 30,000,000 gallons, upon which the duty amounted to about eight millions of pounds sterling.—*Parl. Ret.*

	ACRES.
Waste land in Great Britain and Ireland	15,301,994
Bog land in Ireland	3,000

Square miles of Coal formation in Great Britain	11,859
Tons of Coal produced in 1845	31,500,000
Estimated value at the place of production	£9,450,000

(*World's Progress.*)

	MILES.
Canals in England	2,800
In Ireland	300
Railways in Great Britain in 1850	6,075

Receipts per mile per week, £44. — *American Almanac for* 1850. 5,308 miles have been opened since 1844. The receipts per mile have decreased £20.

Electric Telegraph lines in England in 1849 ...... 2,000 miles.

Vessels in Commerce and Fisheries	23,898
Tonnage	3,007,581

Navy, in 1845	680 vessels.
Army	122,000 men.
Stationed in India	30,000 "

(*Ungewitter.*)

Poor Tax in England in 1845 .... £5,418,845
In Ireland there is no compulsory poor tax.

Universities 3. — London, Oxford, and Cambridge. Oxford has twenty colleges and twenty-five halls; Cambridge, thirteen colleges and four halls.

Instruction to the people in England	1 in 20
" " " Scotland	1 in 11
" " " Ireland	1 in 35

Public Schools for the Poor, exclusive of Sunday Schools.

	Schools.	Scholars.
England	13,642	998,431
Scotland	4,836	181,467
Wales	841	38,164
Ireland	13,327	774,000
	32,646	1,992,062

Public Libraries in Great Britain	53
Volumes	1,780,000

None are taken into account which contain less than ten thousand volumes. — *Parl. Rep. Brit. Mus.*

New books annually printed, exclusive of pamphlets and reprints, fifteen thousand.

Newspapers published in Great Britain in 1849.

London	160
Scotland	232
Ireland	117
English Provinces	94
	603

Advertisements in the London Newspapers in 1849, £886,108; paying a gross duty of £66,453.

The annual revenue from the Penny Post, after paying all expenses, is about £84,000.

There are about three million five hundred houses in England.—*Peter.*

As nearly as can be estimated, the rental of

England, Scotland, and Wales, will amount to about	£34,000,000
Ireland	12,715,478

War absorbs ninety-nine cents of every dollar. — *Sumner.*

Fifteen million pounds annually appropriated for Army and Navy. — *Ib.*

Forty million pounds annual tax to pay for former wars, and to prepare for new. — *Ib.*

Four million pounds annual appropriation for all civil purposes of government. — *Ib.*

Congregations.

Roman Catholics	416
Presbyterians	197
Independents	1840
Baptists	1201
Calvinistic Methodists	427
Wesleyan "	2818
Other "	396

THE END.

LINDSAY & BLAKISTON

PUBLISH

MY LITTLE GEOGRAPHY,

FOR

PRIMARY SCHOOLS AND FOR BEGINNERS.

WITH NUMEROUS ILLUSTRATIONS.

EDITED BY MRS. L. C. TUTHILL.

RECOMMENDATIONS.

From Mrs. E. W. Phelps, Principal of the Female Seminary, Shepherdstown, Jefferson County, Va.

Messrs. Lindsay & Blakiston:—"My Little Geography" is the favourite volume of my younger pupils, who have been charmed with the chapters they have studied, and delighted at finding they could commit the sprightly little verses to memory. Such an elementary treatise was quite a desideratum, and I am pleased that the idea suggested itself to a person capable of carrying it out, in a style so peculiarly adapted to instruct and interest the young.

Very respectfully yours,
E. W. PHELPS.

From J. E. Lovell, Principal of the Lancasterian School, New Haven, Conn.

I have examined a little work, by Mrs. L. C. Tuthill, entitled "My Little Geography." It is by no means an easy task to *write well* for young children, but this performance is, I think, highly successful. Its language is simple and chaste; its sentences concise, and its topics so treated that the youngest pupil will easily understand them. Several books for beginners in Geography—excellent in most respects—have been published within a few years; but they are, without an exception, so far as my knowledge extends, *too comprehensive*, and *above the capacities* of those for whose particular use they were intended. Mrs. Tuthill's little work may be used as introductory to either of them, with great advantage; it will do its own part well, and open the way for the better accomplishment of that which belongs to its successors. I hope it may have an extensive circulation.

J. E. LOVELL.

OPINIONS OF THE PRESS.

This is the title of a captivating little book for children, by which they are led, almost insensibly, into a knowledge of geographical terms.—*Commercial Advertiser.*

Than this unpretending little work we have never seen a more useful or appropriate school-book, or one more admirably calculated for beginners in geography; we can recommend it, without fear of responsibility, to our seminaries, as well deserving a trial.—*Southern Patriot.*

We welcome, with particular pleasure, this little work; the author has succeeded admirably in producing a book which must prove a valuable auxiliary to parents and teachers, as well as a delightful and instructive companion for children.—*Saturday Courier.*

This is an attractive, we must add, entertaining book; as a first Geography for children, it is admirably suited to their capacities, and its embellishments cannot fail to interest them.—*Christian Observer.*

This is a most admirable work for young beginners in Geography; it should be introduced into families and schools.—*Intelligencer and Journal*

LINDSAY & BLAKISTON

PUBLISH

AUNT MARY'S TALES,

BY MRS. HUGHS,

AUTHOR OF "BUDS AND BLOSSOMS," "IVY WREATH," ETC. ETC.

A SERIES OF JUVENILE BOOKS,

FOR

Little Boys and Little Girls.

EACH VOLUME ILLUSTRATED BY A COLOURED FRONTISPIECE.

Ten Volumes, square 16mo.,

CONTAINING AS FOLLOWS:

THE YOUNG ARTIST, OR SELF-CONQUEST.
THE YOUNG SAILOR, OR PERSEVERANCE REWARDED.
HOLIDAYS IN THE COUNTRY, OR VANITY DISAPPOINTED.
GENEROSITY, OR THE STORY OF SYBELLA AND FLORENCE.
THE MOTHER'S BIRTHDAY, OR THE BROKEN VASE.
LISSIE LINDEN, OR HER MOCKING-BIRD.
THE GIPSEY FORTUNE-TELLER, OR THE TROUBADOUR.
FRANK WORTHY; OR THE ORPHAN AND HIS BENEFACTOR.
MAY MORNING, OR A VISIT TO THE COUNTRY.
THE PROUD GIRL HUMBLED, OR THE TWO SCHOOLMATES.

NOTICES OF THE PRESS.

We are glad to see a lady of Mrs. Hughs' abilities so usefully employed. Her stories are written in an engaging style, which will insure their eager perusal, while they convey sound instruction in regard to the improvement of the temper, and the proper cultivation of the domestic and social affections.—*Saturday Courier.*

A series of highly attractive little books for juvenile readers from the pen of Mrs. Hughs, which are happily narrated in a style and manner calculated to awaken an interest in the minds of the young, and blend instruction with amusement, in forms adapted to promote their improvement.—*Christian Observer.*

www.ingramcontent.com/pod-product-compliance
Lightning Source LLC
LaVergne TN
LVHW021411110826
845150LV00007B/1875

* 9 7 8 1 4 2 5 5 1 1 1 9 7 *